Causal Modeling Research on Language Minorities' Achievement

Theoretical Studies in Second Language Acquisition

Simon Belasco
General Editor

Vol. 3

PETER LANG
New York • Washington, D.C./Baltimore
Bern • Frankfurt am Main • Berlin • Vienna • Paris

Lih-Shing Wang

Causal Modeling Research on Language Minorities' Achievement

PETER LANG
New York • Washington, D.C./Baltimore
Bern • Frankfurt am Main • Berlin • Vienna • Paris

Library of Congress Cataloging-in-Publication Data

Wang, Lih-Shing.
Causal Modeling Research on Language Minorities' Achievement/
Lih-Shing Wang.
p. cm. — (Theoretical studies in second languages acquisition; vol. 3)
Includes bibliographical references and index.
1. Academic achievement—United States—Evaluation. 2. Minorities—
Education—United States—Evaluation. I. Series: Theoretical studies in
second language acquisition (New York, N.Y.); vol. 3.
LB1062.6.W36   371.97—dc20   91-43691
ISBN 0-8204-1823-4
ISSN 1051-6670

Die Deutsche Bibliothek-CIP-Einheitsaufnahme

Wang, Lih-Shing.
Causal Modeling Research on Language Minorities' Achievement/
Lih-Shing Wang.
New York; Washington, D.C./ Baltimore; Bern;
Frankfurt am Main; Berlin; Vienna; Paris: Lang.
(Theoretical studies in second language acquisition; vol. 3)
ISBN 0-8204-1823-4
NE: GT

The paper in this book meets the guidelines for permanence and durability
of the Committee on Production Guidelines for Book Longevity
of the Council of Library Resources.

© 1996 Peter Lang Publishing, Inc., New York

Printed in the United States of America.

Dedication

To my parents and my dearest daughter Jennifer

Abstract

The purpose of the present study was to empirically test the validity of a theoretical model linking ethnic-language dominance, socio-economic status, parental involvement to psychological orientation and academic achievement. An unbalanced, multi-group sample was randomly selected from the 1980 High School and Beyond national database. A total of 739 public high school sophomores with complete responses were sampled from three ethnic populations: Asian, Hispanic, and Anglo.

Using linear structural relations (LISREL) modeling as the main analytical procedure, the proposed model was evaluated at three phases. At phase one, a single-group analysis was conducted for each of the three ethnic groups to estimate the factor loadings and structural coefficients. At phase two, a multi-group analysis was used for each pair-wise combination of the three ethnic groups to determine the comparability of the postulated model across groups. At phase three, ethnicity was incorporated into the model for the pooled minority sample to examine the ethnicity effect on school outcomes.

The results confirm some popular theories and suggest alternative ways of thinkings about others: (a) Ethnic-language dominance has a direct negative effect on English achievement, but through the positive effect mediated by psychological orientation it can function as a facilitator of second language learning. (b) Ethnic-language dominance facilitates quantitative learning only to a small extent for Hispanic students; Asian students' superior quantitative achievement in general does not seem to be causally related to their ethnic language status. (c) Socio-economic status effects positive learning directly for the Anglo but only indirectly through psychological orientation for the Asian and Hispanic. (d) Parental involvement has a strong detrimental effect on school learning, which can be nullified only if positive psychological orientation is encouraged. (e) The causal relationship between psychological orientation and academic achievement appears to be primarily uni-directional, with psychological orientation taking causal precedence over achievement.

Both the multi-group analysis and pooled-sample analysis indicate that there is substantial evidence that ethnicity is an important factor in causal modeling research. Any generalization about a generic causal model without due regard to ethnicity should be subject to scrutinization.

Table of Contents

Acknowledgements

This book is based on my doctoral dissertation entitled "A Causal Analysis of Achievement Models for Language Minority Students in the United States: A Linear Structural Relations (LISREL) Approach." I am indebted to all of my committee members at the University of Illinois at Urbana-Champaign for their invaluable guidance throughout the process of my thesis writing. Dr. Delwyn L. Harnisch inspired me of selecting the topic and provided me with the technical assistance. Dr. Lyle F. Bachman helped me formulate the substantive issues and guided me in relating the theory to the methodology. Dr. Maurice M. Tatsuoka provided me with insightful comments on the multivariate statistical analyses of the data. Special thanks go to Dr. James L. Wardrop, my dissertation director, for his assistance in the statistical programming using LISREL. Thanks are also due to my academic advisor, Dr. Gary A. Cziko, who has done an inspiring job in advising my doctoral study.

Lastly, I would like to thank Dr. Simon Belasco for including this study in his "Theoretical Studies in Second Language Acquisition" series. It is my hope that with the addition of this book, we come to better understanding of language minorities' inner world, and thereby providing richer opportunities for learning to all.

Chapter One

Introduction

Statement of the Problem

Attempts to explain academic achievement have traditionally been a central theme in educational research. Many theoretical models have been proposed and much empirical evidence has accumulated, but there remain three major problems with previous research: unjustified inference of causality, inadequate model comprehensiveness, and lack of comparability across ethnic groups.

Causality

Studies designed to explain school performance generally fall into two categories: experimental and observational. Intimidated by the many problems impeding meaningful experiments in education (Cronbach & Snow, 1977), researchers often turn to ecological correlations in observational studies for evidence of causal inference (Lohnes, 1979). In the absence of randomization, temporal precedence, and exhaustive model specification, correlation indices, either full or partial, are at best "suggestive of causal linkages" (Pedhazur, 1982, p. 579).

With the advent of path analysis (Wright, 1934) and structural equation modeling (Jöreskog & Lawley, 1968), coupled with recent advances in efficient parameter estimation and computer software (Jöreskog & Sörbom, 1984; Wold, 1982), researchers now have much more powerful tools to untangle the causal chain.

Causal modeling, however, requires stringent theoretical formulation, advanced mathematical abstraction, and rigorous methodological implementation. Failure to meet the requirements for sound causal studies characterizes many recent endeavors that have utilized the causal modeling approach (see Methodological Review under Review of Literature in this Chapter).

Comprehensiveness

Educational phenomena are without doubt multi-faceted in nature and hierarchical in structure (Bergan, 1980). At the micro level, every theoretical construct can be adequately represented only by multiple manifest variables; at the macro level, any structural model should encompass a full range of relevant causal constructs.

In regression analysis and path analysis, since each construct is represented by a single manifest variable, it is assumed that no measurement error, for the independent variables at least, is involved (Kenny, 1979). This unrealistic assumption of "infallible measurement" has become widely recognized as one of the major limitations of regression and path analysis (Gallini, 1983; Patteson & Wolfle, 1981).

This methodological problem of impractical error-free measurement assumption is further compounded by the frequent omission of relevant constructs in the proposed theoretical framework. Incomplete model specification can result in either reduced explanatory power, biased parameter estimates, or underestimated statistical power (Pedhazur, 1982). Model underspecification of varying degrees is clearly one of the reasons why previous causal studies of educational effectiveness have resulted in inconsistent and inconclusive findings (Foshay & Misanchuk, 1981).

Comparability

Given the diversity of linguistic, social, and psychological orientations among groups of different ethnic backgrounds, it would be erroneous to assume, without empirical evidence, that a "generic" model exists which fits equally well for all ethnic groups. Au (1986), for example, cautioned about the generalizability of the powerful effects of perceived parental expectations to cultures other than the Chinese. Castenell (1983) found vastly different motivational patterns and effects on achievement for blacks and whites. Marjoribanks (1979, 1985) called for different models of family effect on achievement for English-speaking and non-English-speaking groups.

What is needed, then, is a statistical procedure that allows simultaneous parameter estimation of multi-group data, as proposed by Jöreskog (1971) and practiced by Lomax (1985), Sang, Schmitz, Volimer, Baumert, and Roeder (1986), Wolfle and Robertshaw (1983), and Wolfle (1985). To date, only a limited number of research studies have been put forth in testing the validity of causal models across language minority groups.

Significance of the Study

In response to the above stated problems in the area of research on determining educational effectiveness, this study sought to establish a causal model of school outcomes for students of different ethnic backgrounds. The significance of the present study can be approached from three perspectives: the theoretical framework, the analytical framework, and the sampling framework.

The Theoretical Framework

The inclusion of the latent constructs and the operationalization of the indicator variables were carefully weighed against theory and previous research. The existing body of literature in language minority education clearly suggests the importance of ethnic-language dominance, socio-economic status, and parental involvement as determining factors of students' cognitive and psychological development. These variables were therefore included in the postulated achievement models for language minority students in this study.

Other factors such as intelligence, family configuration, and school practices were judged as either irrelevant (Fotheringham & Creal, 1980; Stevenson, Stigler, Lee, Lucker, Kitamura, & Hsu, 1985; Thompson, 1985) or common to all ethnic groups (Biniaminov & Glasman, 1983; Haertel, Walberg, & Weinstein, 1983; Page & Grandon, 1979). These factors were excluded from the present study for two reasons. First, in order to limit the scope of this study to a manageable level, it was necessary to focus on a set of determinants that have been strongly suggested by theory and research to have an influence on achievement. As a result, factors other than linguistic, familial, and psychological were excluded from the proposed achievement models. Second, since one of the major purposes of the present study was to compare models across ethnic groups, these generic causal factors that were expected to affect all groups simultaneously and to a comparable degree were of little interest.

The Analytical Framework

The linear structural relations approach, a procedure for estimating parameters of covariance structure models, was employed as the modeling technique because of its capability of handling both measurement and structural models concurrently in a multivariate setting. Regression analysis is inadequate in that it treats all predictor variables as exogenous and of equal status within the model, disregarding potential or postulated causal structure among them (Wardrop & O'Dell, 1985). Canonical correlation analysis, an extension of multiple regression, is less than ideal in that, much like a zero-order bivariate correlation coefficient, ". . . there is no assumption of causal asymmetry in the mathematics of canonical correlation analysis" (Mardia, Kent, & Bibby, 1979, p. 281). Factorial modeling, akin to confirmatory factor analysis, does not have the capacity to extract in full the structural relationships existing in the data (Lohnes, 1979). Path analysis is also of limited utility in that it does not allow for reciprocal causality, correlated error terms, or partitioning of measurement error (Kenny, 1979).

The linear structural relations approach represents a major improvement over the other statistical procedures in untangling the causal chain of a complex phenomenon. Its versatility in accommodating a large variety of causal models as well as providing equality indices for model comparisons made it the best choice as the analytical procedure for this study.

The Sampling Framework

The data used in this study were randomly drawn from a large-scale national longitudinal study entitled, "High School and

Beyond (HSB)" (National Opinion Research Center [NORC], 1980). Funded by the National Center for Education (NCES) and conducted by the National Opinion Research Center (NORC), the HSB data set represents one of the most valuable national databases available to educational researchers.

Through carefully implemented multistage stratified probability sampling procedures, the HSB data set includes over 58,000 high school students enrolled in 1,015 high schools in the U.S. The representativeness of the HSB sample greatly enhances the external validity of any study utilizing the data set (Miller, 1970).

A major threat to survey research is nonresponse bias (Hartman, Eugua, & Jenkin, 1985-6). The primary concern associated with nonresponse bias is that the non-respondent group often varies systematically from the respondent group on relevant dimensions, prohibiting generalization of research findings to the parent population (Nielsen, Moos, & Lee, 1978). The response rate of the HSB study for schools was 91% and for students, 84% (Peng, Owings, & Fetters, 1982)—both high enough to exclude most concerns over nonresponse bias.

Another issue in survey research is the quality of responses to the questionnaires. By correlating self-reported responses with those reported by outside sources such as schools, teachers, friends, and parents, NCES (1984) reported satisfactory validity coefficients in many important areas. In addition, the reliabilities and difficulty levels of the cognitive tests in the HSB study were also investigated and were found to be appropriate by most conventional standards (Heyns & Hilton, 1982).

It should be evident that the scope and quality of the HSB data set would be difficult, if not impossible, to replicate by any private research parties. By utilizing this highly regarded national resource, the present study minimized the sampling error and measurement error which typically plague research studies similar to the present one.

By operating within the above three frameworks, this study, although observational in nature, "can yield consistent, convincing, useful explanations of educational phenomena" (Cooley, 1978, p. 10).

Review of Literature

The Role of Theory

Theory, as it is often claimed, should be the driving force of any empirical research. The design of a study and the selection of an analysis should be guided by substantive theory rather than by data. Put succinctly by Pedhazur (1982), ". . . an explanatory scheme is not arrived at on the basis of the data, but rather on the basis of knowledge, theoretical formulations and assumptions, and logical analysis (p. 579)."

In examining the literature on language minority education, however, one could easily become frustrated by the scarcity of quality studies and inconsistency of research findings. Particularly difficult is the establishment of direction of causality among latent factors at work. As a result, the initial models proposed for this study, on the basis of previous theory and research, were only tentative and would inevitably undergo a series of empirical verifications (see Analyses in Chapter Two for a detailed description of the initial models). A theory motivates a study to validate the hypothesis derived from it; the result, either falsifying or supporting the hypothesis, in turn shapes or modifies the theory. This interactive and dynamic process, as Fiske (1971) puts it, "is the essence of science (p. 272)."

In the review of literature that follows, I first present a descriptive account of the status of minority achievement, followed by a discussion on the role of English proficiency in determining language minority students' academic achievement. A general review of the hypothesized antecedents of academic achievement is then given, followed by a detailed review of the antecedents of English achievement.

Among the hypothesized antecedents, I first discuss the two causal factors, ethnic-language dominance and socio-economic status, whose determinants were believed to be operating outside the present framework. I then discuss the importance of parental involvement, which functions as a mediating factor between the two causal factors and the two school outcomes—cognitive achievement and psychological orientation.

The primary motive for treating psychological orientation as one of two terminal school outcomes was prompted by the well-documented relationship between psychological orientation and cognitive achievement (Walberg, 1978), as well as the recent attention to socio-emotional adjustment as a measure of educational success (Sue & Zane, 1985). Since the causal paths between cognitive achievement and psychological orientation were hypothesized to be reciprocal, this treatment did not have any effect on the parameter estimation of the model.[1]

Given the significant role of theory in causal modeling, a literature review which exhibits more controversy than consistency would be less than complete without a critical examination of the methodology in previous research. I thus end this section with a methodological review that casts a critical look at the theory and research on which the current model was based.

Cognitive Achievement

A wealth of studies on educational effectiveness has accumulated over the past century. It was not until 1960s, however, that language minorities received attention from educators across the nation (Flores, 1978).

Language minority students, who come from non-English-language backgrounds, have been traditionally viewed as "the disadvantaged" because their academic achievement was commonly observed to be lower than the national norms (Grant & Eiden, 1981). An assumption, either explicitly or implicitly made in these studies, is that ethnicity is related to achievement, and students whose ethnic language is other than English tend to perform poorly in school.

Such a general statement was questioned by Veltman (1980), and he set out to compare the relative educational attainments of black and white children with Hispanic and Asian origins. He found that while children of Hispanic origin tended to have slightly lower than expected attainment level, children from other ethnic origins such as Asian tended to have somewhat higher than expected attainments.

This observation is far from isolated. Many national and international studies of comparative educational achievements consistently reported Asian-origin students outperforming Hispanics and particularly on quantitative measures, Americans (Comber & Keeves, 1973; Stevenson *et al.*, 1985; Husen, 1967; Wang, 1986).

The question of what factors account for the differential achievements both within and across various ethnic groups has been the focus of research interest among many educators in minority issues. One of the most commonly held notions is that academic failure of language minority students is primarily attributable to lack of proficiency in the English language—the medium of formal and informal communication in the English-speaking community (U.S. Commission on Civil Rights, 1975).

Veltman (1980), for example, attributed the observed differential attainments among whites, blacks, and Hispanics to the lack of English proficiency in the Spanish-speaking children. When the limited-English-proficiency students were eliminated from the Hispanic sample, the differences among groups were markedly attenuated.

In characterizing "learning disabled" (LD) students, Shepard, Smith, and Vojir (1983) found more than half of the identified LD group obtained a verbal IQ score significantly lower than the performance IQ. This syndrome was labeled as "language interference" and was asserted to be the cause of academic difficulties among this LD group.

Implicit in these and other studies on linguistic background and minority achievement is the assumption that the relationship between English proficiency and cognitive achievement is a simple, linear, positive one—the higher the English proficiency, the better the academic achievement. Moreover, the causal link between verbal and quantitative achievement is hypothesized to be a nonreciprocal one—verbal achievement is assumed to influence quantitative achievement, but not vice versa.

Before moving on further, a note on "English proficiency" and "verbal achievement" is in order. I have deliberately avoided making a distinction between the two terms. A theoretical treatment of the various dimensions of second language proficiency can be found in Bachman (1990) and Cummins (1982). For all practical purposes of the present study, English proficiency is very broadly defined as the general ability to perform verbal communication in the English language and will be used interchangeably with verbal achievement.

Ethnic-Language Dominance

Perhaps the most heavily researched area in language minority achievement is the role of ethnic language. It is a widely documented belief, for example, that ethnic-language dominance as measured by its frequency, context, and proficiency plays a central role in the person's linguistic, cognitive, and psychological development. Discussed below are three aspects of ethnic-language dominance: use of ethnic language as a child, current use of ethnic language, and length of residence in the U.S.

Use of ethnic language as a child. Whether learning the ethnic language during childhood impedes or accelerates one's later acquisition of another language has been a controversy for over half a century. Early works in minority education seem to regard ethnic language as a negative force competing for the limited available space in the human brain (Jensen, 1962). According to this view, if two languages are allowed to enter that limited space, neither language will fully develop and intellectual confusion will result.

Cummins (1981, 1982), in his thesis of "primary language development," takes the opposite view and argues strongly for the promotion of ethnic language during childhood. In his view, learning the ethnic language at an early age can promote not only literacy skills in both the ethnic language and the English language, but also cognitive development in general.

Current use of ethnic language. An issue related to the use of ethnic language as a child is its continued use in later years. Although never explicitly proposed by any researcher, a theoretical model that advocates the use of the majority language (English) to the exclusion of the ethnic language has prevailed for its intuitive appeal.

A number of studies have provided empirical support for the "home/school linguistic mismatch" hypothesis and placed the blame on language minority students' overreliance on the ethnic language outside the classroom (Iglesia, 1985). It has been demonstrated that the academic disadvantages of language dominance, which in turn is related to their socio-economic status (Laosa, 1984).

Such a claim, however, was quickly disputed by many others. Several studies have shown that retention of ethnic language is not a handicap to academic progress (Ramirez & Politzer, 1976; Yee & La Forge, 1974). An even stronger claim was made by Cummins and Mulcahy (1978) who found that on an English structure test, students who used their ethnic language extensively at home outperformed those who used the majority language exclusively.

In fact, counter-evidence abounds which demonstrates that the use of English at home was actually associated with poor academic performance (Bhatnager, 1980; Chesarek, 1981). Well's (1979) study even pointed out that using the majority language for communication at home, if done in poor quality, could cause detrimental consequences to performance in school.

Length of residence in the U.S. Another heated issue in second language acquisition theory relates to the length of residence in the U.S. The argument is that the longer the exposure to the English-speaking environment, the better chance the student has in making academic progress. Many studies (e.g., Oller, Perkins, & Murakami, 1980; Walberg, Hase, & Rasher, 1978) have given support to this notion and found length of exposure to be a strong predictor of proficiency in the majority language.

However, other studies did not find length of exposure to be a significant predictor of proficiency in the majority language, particularly with older students after puberty (Patkowski, 1980). In fact, some studies even found that language minority students who immigrated to the States at an older age developed significantly better academic skills than native-borns (Baral, 1979; Carter, 1970; Christian, 1976).

The theory behind such observations is that older immigrant students who are exposed to the majority language environment for a shorter period of time tend to be more cognitively mature and their ethnic language proficiency is better developed. As a result, they acquire cognitively demanding aspects of English proficiency more rapidly than younger immigrants

(Genesee, 1978; Krashen, Long, & Scarcella, 1979; Troike, 1978).

It would be, of course, overly simplistic to claim that ethnic-language dominance alone can provide adequate explanation for differential achievements among various ethnic groups. Other than linguistic factors, socio-cultural, psychological, educational, and familial factors all play an important role in the academic development of language minority students (Cheng, 1987). More and more research on minority education has been focusing on these non-linguistic factors such as socio-cultural status and affective variables—a topic we shall now turn to.

Socio-Economic Status

Probably the most well-known non-linguistic factor relating to minority achievement is socio-economic status (SES). As noted by Sowell (1978), ethnicity per se or even language per se are much too general explanations for most of the phenomena dealt with in connection with bilingual education. Differences in home environments, as represented by such characteristics as location, age, income, education or occupation, may explain more of minority achievement than either ethnic membership or language usage.

Echoing Sowell's remarks, Drake (1978) also maintained that social class might have much more explanatory power than ethnicity. As observed by Troike (1978), "at an even more fundamental level, the issue may not be one of language at all, but rather the relative social and cultural status of groups in the community (p. 21)."

Empirical support can be found in Rosenthal, Meline, Ginsburg, and Baker's (1981) study in which it was found that after controlling for SES effect, achievement levels among several language minority groups were not significantly different from each other. So and Chan (1984) used the High School and Beyond data set and found SES and language background to have independent and substantial impact on reading achievement scores.

The importance of SES is evidenced by research on not only minority achievement but also achievement of the general student population. Using a fully recursive path model to examine the effects of race, socio-economic status, and family size on ability, Page and Grandon (1979) found SES to play an influential role on ability. In a review of 28 school input-output surveys, Bridge, Judd, and Moock (1979) also found that among the 35 student, family, peer-group, teacher and school variables, SES contributed significantly to the variation in achievement.

Parental Involvement
Correlational studies have consistently reported positive relationships between parents' attitudes and children's school performance (Chapman & Boersma, 1979). Entwisle and Baker (1983), after partialing out IQ, gender, ethnicity, and children's own expectations, found children's school performance to be significantly correlated with parental expectations. Using multiple regression, Fotheringham and Creal (1980) reported the much more significant role of parental involvement than school practices in predicting academic achievement. Path analysis relating SES, parental expectations to achievement also demonstrated the significant direct and indirect effects of parental expectations on achievement (Seginer, 1986; Song & Hattie, 1984.)

Research on the role of parental involvement in minority students' school performance, however, suggests differential effects of parental involvement in different cultures. Kitano (1974) and Sue (1973) independently proposed that cultures which emphasize obedience to authority and obligation to the family usually "produce" high achievement in school. Since parental authority is a highly regarded virtue in most Asian traditions, it is not surprising that the importance of parental involvement has been repeatedly demonstrated by studies of Asian families (Mace, 1972; Au, 1986).

Psychological Orientation
The role of psychological orientation in second-language acquisition is perhaps best depicted in Krashen's (1982) "Affective Filter Hypothesis." He identified several affective variables such as anxiety, motivation and self-concept related to success in second language acquisition. According to this hypothesis, acquirers in a less-than-optimal affective state (e.g., not motivated) will

have a filter, or mental block, which prevents them from utilizing linguistic input fully for language acquisition.

In relating affective variables directly to academic achievement, Cummins (1982) observed that academic success of minority students was often found to be associated with those who had high "bi-acculturalization"—that is, adapting well linguistically and psychologically to the majority culture while preserving secure identify with their own ethnic language and culture. Chesarek (1981) and Bhatnagar (1980) also report that "acculturated" students who adopted the culture of the majority and switched entirely to the second language demonstrate lower levels of academic achievement than students who maintain their allegiance to their native culture and the use of their ethnic language at home.

Discussed below are three psychological dimensions that have been suggested by the literature to play an influential role in academic achievement: motivation, self-concept, and internal locus of control.

Motivation. One of the most heated debates over the relationship between psychological orientation and academic achievement centers on motivation. In a quantitative synthesis on motivation and achievement, Uguroglu and Walberg (1979) reported a mean correlation of .338 or average explained variance of 11.4%. They concluded that "because of their [motivation and attitudes] replicated correlations with achievement and potential for psychometric improvement, motivation measures clearly deserve inclusion in general research on classroom learning to determine the causal directions and weights for the factors as well as to point to the most effective ways to make learning more productive (p. 387)."

However, the importance of motivation has been challenged by some other empirical studies. Backman (1976), for example, found no significant relationship between motivation/attitudes and second language learning. In a more rigorous study, Fouly (1985) found a structural equation model with the motivation construct eliminated from the model to fit the data significantly better than other models hypothesizing either recursive or nonrecursive paths between motivation and second language proficiency, although the fit was still significantly poor.

For studies that have found motivation to be an important factor, there is little consensus as to the direction of casuality. Lambert (1967) theorized that a learner's attitudes and motivation toward the target group determined success in learning the target language. Elaborating on Lambert's theory, Gardner's (1979) earlier work confirmed that motivation determined second language acquisition, less so the other way around.

Other studies, however, reported the causal predominance of achievement over motivation. Savignon (1972) found that among learners who initially had expressed no particular desire to learn French, the higher achievers were more likely to express a desire to continue their study than the lower achievers. Herman (1980) observed that advanced students had significantly higher level of positive attitudes toward the target culture; thus achievement was believed to cause motivation, not vice versa. Based on similar observations, Strong (1984) and Burstall, Jamieson, Cohen, and Hargreaves (1974) also asserted that motivation was a result, rather than the cause, of achievement.

Still others supported bi-directional causality between motivation and achievement. Harmers and Blanc (1982) proposed a socio-psychological model for the development of bilingualism, in which they hypothesized the interdependence between motivation and linguistic and cognitive development in both languages. Gardner, Lalond, and Pierson (1983), in examining the causal linkages between attitudes, motivation, and second language achievement, among others, found motivation and achievement to influence each other. Similar findings were also reported in Fouly's (1985) study in which he found that the model with bi-directional causality between motivation and second language proficiency fit the data significantly better than the models with uni-directional paths between the two constructs.

Self-concept. The literature on self-concept exhibits no less contradictory results than the literature on motivation and achievement. In a meta-analysis by Hansford and Hattie (1982), correlations between self-concept and achievement ranged from $-.77$ to $.96$, with a mean of $.21$ and average explained variance of $.05$. A causal analysis by Pottbaum, Keith, and Ehly

(1986) reported no significant causal relation between self-concept and academic achievement in a cross-lagged panel correlation design. They concluded that a third variable may be causally predominant over both self-concept and achievement.

Among those studies that did find self-concept to be a causal factor, there is little agreement as to the causal ordering. Scheirer and Kraut (1979) reviewed the research bearing on the causal predominance of self-concept and concluded that there was no support for the proposition that changes in self-concept caused changes in achievement and suggested that "self-concept change is likely to be an outcome of increased achievement with accompanying social approval, rather than an intervening variable necessary for achievement to occur (p. 144)."

Anderson and Evans (1974), however, employed recursive causal modeling procedure and found a strong direct effect of self-concept on achievement. Using cross-lagged nonrecursive panel modeling, Shavelson and Bolus (1982) also reported causal predominance of self-concept over achievement. Song and Hattie (1984), based on cross-validated Korean samples, found further support for strong positive direct effect of academic self-concept on achievement and asserted that home environment (family configuration, SES, parental characteristics) had only indirect effect on achievement mediated by self-concept.

Locus of control. Research on locus of control, alternatively termed "causal attribution",[2] has unanimously pointed to its positive relationship with academic achievement. Dweck (1975), for example, has shown that low internal locus of control resulted in learned helplessness, which in turn caused low performance. In a regression study, Willig, Harnisch, Hill, and Maehr (1983) found significant predictive power of causal attributions on math achievement, and the significance was higher for the Black and Anglo samples than the Hispanic sample.

From a broader perspective of social-cultural power relations, language minority students, being "dominated" by the majority group, internalize their inferior status. This perceived "dispowerment" predisposes minority children to school failure even before they come to school (Ogbu, 1978). As a remedy, Cummins (1986) suggested ways to "empower" minority students in order to avoid academic failure.

Methodological Review

The above review of the literature on language minority achievement probably leaves one with more questions than answers. Very different findings have been reported as to the strengths and directions of the relationships between the various background variables and academic achievement.

This should not be too surprising since not equally rigorous methodological control was exercised in all the studies cited. Dulay and Burt (1978), for example, rejected 95% of the reports they surveyed for failure to meet methodological standards. Fouly (1985) also presented an excellent discussion on the possible sources of contamination that contributed to contradictory findings.

Because of its theoretical appeal and software availability, causal modeling has received wide popularity in the past decade. However, the mere application of this modeling procedure does not guarantee establishment of causation or proof of theory of any sort. Unthoughtful implementation and unsubstantiated interpretation lead to the misuse and abuse of various causal modeling approaches. Discussed below are some common weaknesses that were exhibited in many causal studies reviewed above.

Model/analysis mismatch. The most profound problem with studies claiming to determine the causal forces of some educational phenomena is the inadequacy of the analysis procedure employed for testing the research model. A frequently cited case of model/analysis mismatch is the use of regression, analysis of variance, or some variation of both in nonexperimental research in the attempt to draw causal inference. Examples of such misapplication abound.

To illustrate, Herman (1980) and Strong (1984) independently studied the relationship between motivation and second language proficiency. Having found that the advanced group showed significantly higher level of motivation than the beginning group, they concluded that achievement caused motivation, not vice versa. Such a claim not only oversimplifies the complex framework of second language acquisition, but also totally disregards the equally plausible conclusion that high motivation may have contributed to the high proficiency status of the advanced group.

An equally simple-minded assertion is the negative effect of home/school linguistic mismatch based on the observation that language minority students who experienced school failure tend to be those who speak a different household language from English (Schneider, 1976; Shepard *et al.*, 1983). More and more evidence has emerged that suggests other more fundamental causes at work (Marjoribanks, 1979; Page & Grandon, 1979). Only when non-ethnic-language factors are controlled for can a study assert the effect of ethnic language.

Other studies that attempted to examine the "overall picture" of causal effects on educational performance turned to multiple regression (e.g., Thompson, 1985). Although multiple regression can easily accommodate a dozen or more independent variables for predicting a single dependent variable, it tends to obscure not only the potential causal ordering but also the possible hierarchical clustering among the independent variables. Thus, although regression analysis is an excellent tool for predictive research, without strong theoretical and statistical assumptions, it lends little explanatory support in causal studies.

Among those studies that did employ a causal modeling technique of one kind or another, few are without problems. Take path analysis for example. Path analysis, among other things, assumes "infallible measurement" since each construct being measured by a single indicator variable is assumed to be perfect representation of itself. At the theoretical level, the use of a single indicator for a potentially complex educational construct is logically indefensible (Foshay & Misanchuk, 1981). At the technical level, by assuming infallible measurement the parameter estimation procedure fails to partition the specific error from the common variance (Lomax, 1986), resulting in biased parameter estimates (Patteson & Wolfle, 1981).

An opposite situation may occur when the researcher includes too many indicator variables in the path model, each claiming to measure a distinct but correlated construct (e.g.,

Shavelson & Bolus, 1982). This practice ignores the possible existence of a higher-order common latent construct and fails to provide, as Lohnes (1979) puts it, "a formal, parsimonious abstraction of reality, phrased in terms of hypothesized orthogonal causes and parameterized by the coefficients for those causes in linear structural equations for all the measurement variates (p. 328)."

Another common critique of path analysis is its inability to handle nonrecursive models. Parkerson, Lomax, Schiller, and Walberg (1984) used LISREL to test a series of recursive models relating home environment, social environment, motivation, among other things, to achievement. Besides many other methodological flaws, their failure to simultaneously estimate possible reciprocal paths may well have been one reason for the poor fit.

Seginer (1986) used recursive path analysis to test one-way linkage from SES, mother's expectations and supporting behaviors to achievement. Without even reporting any goodness-of-fit indices, he concluded that his data supported the hypothesis that achievement-related behaviors transmitted educational expectations and directly affected achievement. Again, as he himself realized, an examination of the reciprocal influences of parents' practices and children's outcomes may have produced more valid results.

A natural extension of path analysis that can test nonrecursive path models is simultaneous-equations modeling (Wolfle, 1980). It differs from the ordinary least-squares (OLS) estimation of recursive path models in that when a relation is part of a simultaneous system, some regressors are stochastic and may be correlated with the regression disturbance (Kmenta, 1971); as a result, OLS estimates are inconsistent. Alternatively, two-stage least squares (TSLS) estimates can yield consistent and less biased estimates, although the variance of the estimates tends to be larger and consequently less efficient (Rao & Miller, 1971).

Several studies have successfully utilized simultaneous equations modeling for testing nonrecursive path models (e.g., Mason & Halter, 1971; Robinson, 1985). However, some of the studies that used this modeling technique failed to realize that

TSLS yielded inconsistent estimates of the standard errors when the endogenous variable was dichotomous and therefore its error term was heteroscedastic.

The studies by Heckman and MaCurdy (1984) and Pascarella and Chapman (1983) exemplify such a case in which they dichotomized the withdrawal/persistence variable but carried out usual TSLS estimation procedure without correcting for the heteroscedasticity as suggested by Heckman and MaCurdy (1984). It is not surprising that they found weak explanatory power of their model and were forced to conclude that "perhaps a major portion of persistence/withdrawal behavior is so idiosyncratic . . . that it is difficult to capture in any rational explanatory model" (Pascarella & Chapman, 1983, p. 99).

Assumption of multivariate normal distribution. The linear structural relations approach represents a powerful and versatile extension of the path analysis. The most commonly used estimation method in this approach is maximum likelihood (ML), whose power and versatility, however, are gained at the price of some stringent assumptions. One of them is the assumption of multivariate normal distribution when the maximum likelihood estimation procedure is used for minimizing the fitting function (Jöreskog, 1967). This assumption offers a general framework for (a) maximum likelihood estimation, (b) hypothesis testing of the model, and (c) estimation and assessment of standard errors for the parameters (Sellin, 1986).

Although ML parameter estimation is fairly robust to moderate departures from normality, caution must be exercised in interpreting the standard errors, particularly when measurement errors are sizeable (Jörekog & Sörbom, 1984). When there is reason to suspect the multivariate normality of the joint distribution, formal test of significance should be carried out as suggested by Gnanadesikan (1977). When in practicality constructing a "good" overall test of joint normality is infeasible (Johnson & Wichern, 1982, p. 151), either a preliminary test of univariate normal distribution is highly desirable (Fouly, 1985), or an alternative modeling technique that is distribution-free should be sought (Wold, 1982).

Unfortunately, too many studies have blindly applied the linear structural relations approach to their data without the least regard to this important distributional assumption. As a consequence, the validity of their conclusions based on any significance tests may be subject to question.

Operationalization. How the latent constructs are conceptualized and how the indicator variables are operationalized play a decisive role in determining the validity and generalizability of a causal modeling study. Different theoretical conceptualizations and empirical operationalization procedures in different studies may well explain why inconsistent conclusions in the minority achievement literature have been drawn.

Consider, for example, ethnic-language dominance. Research on the causal relationship between ethnic-language dominance and academic achievement varies substantially in the dimension of ethnic-language dominance the researcher chose to investigate. Moore and Smith (1985) looked only at whether the "household language" was English or non-English, and how the dichotomous status related to mathematics aptitude. Along a similar vein, Robinson (1985) examined the effect of mother tongue maintenance (retention of a non-English language as home language) on educational and occupational outcomes. Mother tongue maintenance was again dichotomized as either retention or non-retention of the mother tongue in the home.

In another study that looked at the relationship between ethnic language ability and second language proficiency, Nelson, Lomax, and Perlman (1984) operationalized "first language cognitive ability" by an instrument given in the native language (Spanish) "designed for evaluating the backgrounds of individuals who have attended teacher preparatory institutions where the instruction is primarily in Spanish (p. 33)."

Purcell (1983) took yet another perspective in examining the causal models of second language pronunciation accuracy: he dichotomized the first language variable based on whether the subject was a Persian/Arabic or Thai/Japanese. Sang *et al.* (1986) presented a more "traditional" way of defining first language ability—by administering an instrument designed to measure first language skills such as spelling, pronunciation, lexical knowledge, and text comprehension.

The same observation of diverse perspectives involved in operationalization can be said about other hypothesized non-linguistic causal constructs in educational performance. A glance at Song and Hattie's (1984) study should give a convincing picture of the chaotic status of operationalization. In a carefully designed and cross-validated causal model, they demonstrated vastly differential effects of various dimensions of self-concept (academic, social, personal) on academic achievement. Depending on the dimensions chosen by the researchers, different conclusions as to the causal relations between self-concept and achievement would have been drawn.

Before leaving the subject of operationalization, I would like to elaborate further on operationalizing the construct of second language proficiency. Because of its unique relevance to causal models of language minority achievement, the "dimensionality" issue of second language proficiency construct warrants a closer review.

In the 1960's when behavioristic psychology, structural linguistics, and audio-lingual pedagogy were at their peaks, language was regarded primarily as a system of discrete linguistic skills (listening, speaking, reading, and writing) and components (vocabulary, grammar, pronunciation, etc.). In the 1970's the construct validity of such a "divisible language hypothesis" was seriously challenged by a series of empirical work (e.g., Flahive, 1980), and "unitary language proficiency" was proclaimed as a "psychologically real" entity (Oller, 1980).

Following the emergence of the unitary language hypothesis, a number of LISREL-type studies were conducted to challenge the claim. Purcell (1983) found that a two-oblique-factor model, one representing formal language learning and the other informal language acquisition, best accounted for second language pronunciation accuracy, thus rejecting the existence of an all-inclusive unitary factor.

Purcell's findings, even if they could be methodologically justified, by no means offers a settlement of the unitary versus divisible language controversy. The reason is simple: he misconceptualized the theoretical construct of language proficiency, which was the heart of the issue. For one thing, the two distinct but correlated factors he found represented background influences rather than theoretical dimensions of the language construct. For another, language proficiency was very narrowly defined as "pronunciation accuracy," which was clearly a far-from-adequate representation of the latent construct. His study illustrates an extreme case of inadequate operationalization.

Another study that exhibits misoperationalization of the language construct is by Sang *et al.* (1986). In their attempts to falsify the unitary language hypothesis, they "constructed", literally, three-factors—elementary (basic elements of knowledge), complex (integration of basic knowledge), and communicative (integrative use of language). As their names implied, these postulated dimensions were ordered "hierarchically" and each successive skill presupposed the mastery of its preceding skill(s). The authors then assigned seven measures to the three postulated factors, based not on the theoretical dimensions of language but on their perceived difficulty levels in the hierarchical ordering. This procedure, I would argue, "forced" the emergence of a statistical artifact—a three-factor model—to fit the data well.

A much more theoretically justifiable approach would be to use an exploratory factor analysis to inspect the natural clustering of the language measures, followed by a confirmatory factor analysis to examine the fit of the resulting factor model. The operational model proposed and tested by Fouly (1985) postulated three language dimensions (aural/oral, structure/reading, discourse) based not on perceived difficulty but on a theoretical framework (Bachman, 1990). His findings that both a correlated-trait model and a higher-order general factor with three first-order traits fit the data equally well lend strong empirical support to Carroll's (1983) contention: ". . . neither the 'unitary' nor the 'divisible' hypothesis in its extreme is supported, but that language proficiency has both unitary and divisible aspects (p. 87)."

The important implication of the above review on the dimensionality of second language proficiency is that in a structural model such as the one proposed in this study which involves a second language construct, a general latent factor with several distinct but correlated language measures should be theoretically well grounded.

Reliability and validity of measurement model. The detrimental effect of measurement error, or alternatively, unreliability of the measurement model in causal modeling is well documented (Walker & Lev, 1952). Patteson and Wolfle (1981), for example, found that least squares regression estimates would be biased by substantial amounts when compared to estimates adjusted for the presence of measurement error.

In a simulation study in which the values of reliability were systematically manipulated, Lomax (1986) was able to demonstrate how the parameter estimates changed as a result of differing levels of reliability. Specifically, when reliability (specific variance) decreased, error variance for that variable increased systematically since specific and error variances were inversely related; the remaining parameters of the measurement model remained unchanged; the ML estimate and standard error for the relevant structural coefficient increased at the same rate; the ML estimate of the disturbance variance also decreased; and goodness of fit of the model was unchanged.

What solutions, then, are available for the measurement error problem? A common solution for the path models has been to correct the sample correlation coefficients for unreliability (Lord & Novick, 1968) and then utilize the disattenuated coefficients as the input for estimating the structure coefficients (Fuller & Hidiroglou, 1978). This procedure, however, has come under attack: ". . . in the absence of multiple measurements [this procedure] required *a priori* knowledge of the reliability coefficients for the variables; furthermore, one had to assume the reliabilities were invariant from one population, subpopulation or sample to the one at hand" (Wolfle & Robertshaw, 1983, p. 39).

A better solution is to obtain multiple measures of each latent factor, and by so doing partition the error associated with the measurements in the estimation. The resulting parameter estimates are thus disattenuated for the unreliabilities in the measured variables (Kenny, 1979).

Turning to the application studies using casual modeling approach, one sees either complete neglect of the reliability issue (e.g., Nelson *et al.*, 1984), or low reliabilities reported without due regard to their detrimental effects on parameter estimates (Parkerson *et al.*, 1984; Pascarella & Chapman, 1983).

The validity of a measurement model is a less addressed issue in the evaluation of causal models. Dillon and Goldstein (1984) introduced a "shared variance measure" defined as the ratio of the variance captured by the construct over that variance plus the variance due to measurement error. A ratio of less than .50 is indicative of low validity of the measurement model.

Overall model-data fit. Among several alternative measures of model-data fit (Jöreskog & Sörbom, 1984), chi-square statistic is the most often used test in evaluating the validity of the overall model. However, there are many problems associated with the chi-square test: (a) Chi-square is very sensitive to departures from multivariate normal distribution and large sample size (Olsson & Bergman, 1977), (b) Chi-square is only valid for overidentified models since a just-identified model will always fit the data perfectly (Dillon & Goldstein, 1984), and (c) A low and nonsignificant chi-square may imply low and nonsignificant variable relationships in the model. That is, week observed variable relationships increase the probability of obtaining a good fit (Dillon & Goldstein, 1984).

As a consequence of the inappropriateness of the chi-square test, many other goodness-of-fit measures have been suggested: goodness-of-fit index (GFI), root mean square residual (RMSR), and normalized residuals (Jöreskog & Sörbom, 1984). Bentler and Bonett (1980) also suggested a fit statistic that is not a function of sample size. Another approach is to compute the chi-square/df ratio; a ratio of less than 5 would indicate an adequate fit (Wheaton, Muthen, Alwin, & Summers, 1977); a value of less than 1, however, would indicate overidentifiability (Schmitt, 1978). Lastly, the squared multiple correlation (SMC) for each of the structural equations and the total coefficient of determination for all the structural equations jointly provide a good estimate of the overall model-data fit.

Having reviewed the relative strengths and weaknesses of the various model-data fit indices, we can now turn to the literature for the appropriateness in the reporting of model evaluation. Some studies reported only multiple R-square (Page &

Grandon, 1979; Keith & Page, 1985); some reported multiple R-square and residuals (Pascarella & Chapman, 1983; Seginer, 1986); others relied on chi-square exclusively and found unacceptable fit (Nelson *et al.*, 1984; Parkerson *et al.*, 1984); still others found significant chi-square but reported reasonably high multiple-R square to support their findings (Purcell, 1983; Shavelson & Bolus, 1982). A number of studies used the chi-square/df ratio for assessing fit after having found a significant chi-square (Gardner *et al.*, 1983; Song & Hattie, 1984). A few also looked at multiple-R square, residuals, in addition to chi-square and chi-square/df ratio (Fouly, 1985; Sang *et al.*, 1986).

It should be evident that none of the goodness-of-fit measures alone can provide adequate evaluation of the overall model-data fit. A combination of multiple measures is highly desirable when reporting the modeling results.

Specification search. It is an exception rather than the norm to find the initial model suggested by theory to fit the data adequately. Given that the initial model has been rejected, there may be little theoretical guidance as to how the model can be improved. A number of empirical methods are available in searching for a better-fitting model. One is to eliminate non-significant paths as indicated by a t- or z- test, thereby recovering degrees of freedom and increasing the critical value for rejecting the model (Lomax, 1983). Another is to free a fixed parameter whose modification index is greater than 3.84, indicating that appreciable gain will likely result from freeing that parameter (Long, 1983a). Based on either or both of the above indices, the improvement of the model can then be evaluated by the chi-square differences.

There are, however, several problems with such empirical search for better fitting models if done in a purely exploratory, data-driven fashion. For one thing, it is not unusual for a researcher who relied too much on "automatic modification" without due regard to theory to come up with a final model totally detached from theory. Such "theory trimming" (Heise, 1969) is a dangerous practice since it leads to capitalizing on the idiosyncratic nature of the sample at hand. This is why Leamer (1978) suggests that the same data should not be used in the process of specification search. Modification and verification should be made with a second, independent sample.

A related but less discernible problem is when the model cannot be falsified. Consistency of the model with the data does not constitute proof of a theory; at best it lends support to it, and it does not rule out the possibility of other equally plausible models. When competing models are supported by the data, the decision as to which of them is more tenable rests not on the data but rather on the theory that generated the model in the first place (Pedhazur, 1982).

With the above warnings in mind, we now turn to the literature for examples of unjustified theory trimming in the process of specification search.

Gardner and his associates (Gardner, 1979; Gardner *et al.*, 1983; Gardner, Lalonde & MacPherson, 1985) conducted a series of research on the social-educational model of second language acquisition. Their work has very significant bearing on second language theory in that theirs was the pioneering work in model-based studies that utilized the LISREL approach to provide empirical support to second language learning/ acquisition theories (Cummins, 1981; Krashen, 1982; Lambert, 1967).

Their initial model hypothesized causal linkage among cultural beliefs, initial French achievement, language attitudes, motivation, and situational anxiety to final French achievement. Following Lomax's (1982) suggestion on the procedure for model modification, they claimed that all their modification decisions were made without the "personal preferences of the investigator intervening (p. 10)."

Such blatant empiricism, however, led to several theoretically questionable conclusions regarding some of the postulated paths. For example, for lack of significance, they concluded that there was no causal relationship (either uni-directional or bi-directional) between initial achievement and motivation and between anxiety and final achievement.

The claim that no relationship exists between initial achievement and motivation is difficult to justify when it is contrasted with the demonstrated causality between motivation and final achievement in the same study.[3] Such contradictory findings, then, would have to be explained by some idiosyncratic nature of the sample or the context of the study, as the authors themselves acknowledged (p. 12), and therefore contribute little to our understanding of the causal relationship between motivation and achievement.

In their attempt to explain why initial achievement was found to cause anxiety but no relationship was found between anxiety and final achievement, they argued that it was the unique cultural milieu of the study that precluded a causal link between anxiety and final achievement (p. 13), and that their findings should not be taken as evidence against the theoretical model which hypothesized that anxiety acts as a causal determinant of subsequent achievement (Clement, 1980). However, if indeed the cultural milieu of their study had obscured the causal relationship between anxiety and final achievement, we would expect the same to have happened between initial achievement and anxiety.

It can be seen that their overreliance on data-driven empiricism had led them into drawing theoretically ungrounded conclusions. That very different measures were used for operationalizing the initial and final achievement might have provided a better explanation than what they have suggested.[4]

An extreme case of inappropriate theory trimming is demonstrated in Parkerson *et al.*'s (1984) study on educational achievement. In a totally exploratory study, they tested five causal models linking home environment, peer group, media, ability, social environment, time on task, motivation, and instructional strategies to achievement. No theoretical justification was provided for the construction of any of the five models. Such exploratory use of the confirmatory LISREL procedure yielded a final model which was based exclusively on the empirical data and was found to be only marginally statistically acceptable (chi-square/df = 52.6/17 = 3.09, p < .0001),[5] considering the small sample size (N = 39).

Operating in the absence of theory, they failed in three critical stages of their specification search: They failed to provide theoretical framework for their initial model, they failed to provide theoretical justification for their intermediate models, and they failed to provide theoretical interpretation for their final model.

Many other studies shared weaknesses similar to those discussed above. For example, Pascarella and Chapman (1983) and Seginer (1986) reported their final models (which may still have not had acceptable fit) without even discussing how their final models were arrived at. It seems reasonable to assume that those who chose not to report their modification process or simply neglected the importance of reporting it have done their specification search in a purely data-driven manner.

One last note on model evaluation in the specification search process: A not-often-articulated condition for evaluating competing structural models is that the number of constructs in each of the models being compared should be the same; otherwise the model with fewer constructs is always likely to fit the data better because of the reduction in degrees of freedom (Linn, personal communication, 1984).

Fouly (1985) compared four competing models: one with a causal link from motivation to achievement, one with a causal link from achievement to motivation, one with a reciprocal link between motivation and achievement and lastly a model with motivation completely eliminated. Not surprisingly, he found a significant chi-square improvement for the last model over the first three—a statistical artifact disguised in the game of specification search.

A similar problem exists in the evaluation of competing measurement models. It requires little expertise in factor analysis to realize that the more factors extracted, the higher the percentage of variance explained. It should come as no surprise that Shavelson and Bolus (1982) found a model for self-concept with eight correlated factors to explain the variance best compared to the one-factor and two-factor models. A more sensible approach would be to compare the eight-factor model with a hierarchical model that hypothesizes the same number of first-order factors plus one or more second-order factors.

Finally, researchers should guard against the temptation to explore different causal orderings with the same set of data in order to optimize the goodness of fit (Duncan, 1970). It has been suggested that model specification should be conducted on a second independent sample (Leamer, 1978). However, one may test alternative models with the same set of data if and only if the alternative models are proposed prior to the analysis of data (Griffin, 1977). Unfortunately, very few studies reviewed above have put this constraint into practice.

Model comparability. In the situation where the research interest is to compare the magnitudes of structural coefficients among groups, conducting single-sample analysis for each group individually yields little knowledge as to the statistical significance of the discrepancies.

Jöreskog (1971) describes a systematic approach for multi-group comparison: by testing the invariance of factor structure in a hierarchical order. If an equality constraint results in a significant deterioration in the fit of the model, the null hypothesis and all its subsequent invariance hypotheses are disconfirmed and the groups are judged to be dissimilar at that and all subsequent levels. (See the section on Analyses in Chapter Two for more detailed discussion.)

Studies using multi-group LISREL analysis have generally followed Jöreskog's suggestion for testing model comparability to a satisfactory extent (e.g., Wolfle & Robertshaw, 1983). A major problem, though, is again the exploratory use of LISREL for multi-group analysis. As done in Lomax's (1985) study which compared the structural models of public and private schools, a series of varying degrees of equality constraints were imposed on the two groups, and a final model constructed from all the intermediate models was reported without any reference to theoretical justification.

Another common problem in multi-group analysis is that the decision to impose subsequent equality constraints in the hierarchical sequence was often made without reference to significance tests. Take Lomax's (1985) study for example. For each model of varying degree of equality constraint he reported the normed fix index (p. 224, Table 6) representing the degree of improvement in fit over the initial null model. Upon discovering that the model with both the factor loadings and the measurement errors set to be equal (Model 6) yielded a smaller normed fix index than the previous model with only factor loadings set to be equal (Model 5), he was quick to conclude that public school students and private school students were invariant in their factor loadings, but their measurement errors were not.

The question he failed to address was whether the drop in the normed fit index from Model 5 to Model 6 (0.012) represented a statistically significant deterioration in fit. If the drop was found to be of insignificant magnitude, then the conclusion that public and private school students had differential measurement errors would not have been upheld.

Still other studies either failed to report any statistics on model comparability (e.g., Sang *et al.*, 1986), or did not even bother to use simultaneous multi-group analysis when making group comparisons (e.g., Keith & Page, 1985).

It should be evident from the above critical review of methodology that causal modeling is still very much an ill-practiced methodology in educational research. It was these methodological weaknesses that this study sought to avoid in its hope to advance our understanding of the educational process of the American youth.

Statement of Hypotheses

Presented below are the hypotheses tested in this study. More detailed descriptions of the analyses can be found in Chapter Two under the Analyses section.

Phase One: Single-Group Analysis
1. Six latent constructs (ethnic-language dominance, socio-economic status, parental involvement, psychological orientation, verbal and quantitative achievements) exert significant effects on each other following the postulated causal ordering for each of the three ethnic groups (Hispanic, Asian, and Anglo).
2. The proposed model, after being subjected to theoretically justifiable empirical modifications, provides adequate fit to the data for each of the three ethnic groups.

Phase Two: Multi-Group Analysis
3. The optimal-fitting model for the language minority students is not invariant between Hispanic and Asian students. The var-

ious causal factors exert differential effects on school outcomes among the two language minority groups.

4. The optimal-fitting model for the Anglo students is less deviant from that of the Asian than from the Hispanic. In other words, the Anglo model fits the Asian student data better than the Hispanic student data, primarily due to the more comparable status between the Anglo and Asian students.

Phase Three: Pooled-Sample Analysis
5. Ethnicity accounts for significant differences in school outcomes for the pooled language minority group (Hispanic and Asian combined) in the postulated causal ordering.

Definitions of Key Terms

This section only provides brief definitions of the key terms and variables included in this study. For detailed description on the operationalization of the variables, please refer to the sections on Subjects and Variables in Chapter Two.

Terms Related to Ethnicity
1. *Majority language* or *second language*. This term refers to the primary language used in the context of this study—the United States. The majority language thus refers to English in this study.

2. *Ethnic language* or *minority language*. This term refers to the language spoken by the community members of the family origin. This should be carefully distinguished from the term "native language" or "mother tongue," which refers to the first language a person learned as a child. A native-born Chinese American, for example, may have learned English as his or her first language but the ethnic language would be Chinese.

Note also that ethnic language is not necessarily the "home language" or "household language" since ethnic language may, under rare circumstances, no longer be spoken in the home but still spoken in other contexts.

3. *English-language background*. This term refers to the family origins where English is the official language. For example,

students whose families came from Britain or Australia would be considered English-language background origins (see exceptions below.)

4. *Non-English-language background.* This term refers to the family origins in which a language other than English is used as the official language. For example, students whose families came from Korea or Mexico would be considered non-English language background origins.

Exceptions to this identification scheme are students from countries of colonial history such as the Philippines and India, where English is the official language but were considered non-English background origins in this study. If those students indicated no extensive use of a non-English language, however, they would be excluded from the present study.

5. *Language majorities.* This term refers to persons in the United States whose family origins are from English-language backgrounds *and* who have never made extensive use of a non-English language. Accordingly, a person who came from an English-language background but for some reason picked up a non-English language and made extensive use of it in various contexts (e.g., home, work, community) would not be considered a language majority, neither would he or she be considered a language minority. Such a person would simply be excluded from the present study.

As another example, a person who came from an English-language background and who studied a non-English language as a school subject would normally be considered a language majority unless the person was so addicted to the language that he or she used it not only in school but also at home or at work. Such a person would be excluded from the present study.

6. *Language minorities.* This term refers to persons in the United States whose family origins are from non-English backgrounds *and* whose ethnic language is still used extensively in one or more contexts such as school or home.

It is important to note that, according to these criteria, blacks are considered language majorities rather than language minorities (but are not included in this study for their distinct cultural background from whites). In addition, it is possible for a student to be native speaker of English (i.e., learned English as the first language) but still considered language minority.

7. *Ethnic-language dominance.* This term defines the extent to which a language minority is dominated by his or her ethnic language as measured by the frequency of the ethnic language use, the contexts where the ethnic language is used, the amount of exposure to the majority language environment, and the general ethnic language proficiency in listening, speaking, reading, and writing.

Terms Related to Latent Constructs

1. *School outcomes.* This term refers to school performance as measured by both cognitive and psychological tests. Although not necessarily good measures of schooling effect in a strict sense, they are nevertheless valued outcomes in the educational process.

2. *Cognitive achievement.* The term "cognitive" refers to both verbal and quantitative abilities as measured by objective tests in the English language. The term "achievement" is used in a very general sense to encompass the following: ability, proficiency, and attainment.

3. *Psychological orientation.* This terms refers to the degree of affective adaptation or adjustment to the school environment. Among the many facets of psychological orientation discussed in the literature, three were included in this study: motivation, self-concept, and internal locus of control (see "Variables Included in the Model" below for brief definitions of these measures).

Variables Included in the Model

Brief definitions of the eighteen indicator variables for the six latent constructs are given in Table 1. Detailed discussions of those variables can be found in Chapter Two.

Limitations of the Study

Several limitations in this study which may negatively affect the validity and generalizability of the present study are discussed below.

Table 1
Definitions of Key Variables

Construct	Variable	Definition
Ethnic-Language Dominance		
	ELCHILD	Use of ethnic language as a child: Degree of monolingualism during childhood
	CURREL	Current use of ethnic language: Frequency of current ethnic-language use
	YRSUS	Years in U.S.: Length of residence in the U.S.
	ELABL	Self-reported general ethnic-language ability
Socio-Economic Status		
	PAROCC	Parents' current occupational status
	PARED	Parents' highest educational level
	INCOME	Annual family income
	POSSESS	Quality and quantity of household possessions
Parental Involvement		
	PARSCHL	Parental monitoring of school work and life
	PARPLAN	Parental planning of high school program
Psychological Orientation		
	CONCPT	Self-Concept: Perceived image toward self
	CONTRL	Internal locus of control: Perceived power over environment
	MOT	Motivation: Attitude and aspiration toward schooling
Verbal Achievement		
	VOCAB	Performance on the 21-item vocabulary test
	READING	Performance on the 20-item reading test
	WRITING	Performance on the 17-item writing test
Quantitative Achievement		
	MATH	Performance on the 38-item math test
	SCIENCE	Performance on the 20-item science test

Attrition

Attrition effect presents a constant threat to research on minority groups. It is a well-documented fact that language minority students are more than twice as likely as their English-language background counterparts to drop out before high school (Nielsen & Fernandez, 1981; Rumbarger, 1983; Waggoner, 1981). As cautioned by So (1983), since the HSB data set surveyed only high school sophomores and seniors, the sample was likely to be biased in that only the talented or determined language minority students were included in this study.

Operationalization

Operationalization of some of the eighteen variables presented special difficulty since the data were collected by a third party for purposes not designed specifically for this study. In this sense, the present study was "confined" to whatever information was available in the original data source.

Take ELCHLD (use of ethnic language as a child) as an example. This variable was constructed from two survey items: (a) "What was the first language you spoke when you were a child?" and (b) "What other language did you speak when you were a child?" A crude measure of childhood monolingualism constructed from these two items may not be a reliable indicator.

Another constraint is that potentially useful information had to be dropped from the present study because of the difficulty involved in operationalizing the constructs. For example, it would have been of interest to study the effect of bilingual schooling on achievement. The items on the survey relating to bilingual education asked whether the student took bilingual courses in grades 1-6 and 7-9 respectively. The validity of such a crude measure is certainly open to question and was therefore dropped from the study.

Survey Research

Although a generally well designed survey study, the HSB study suffered from at least three methodological weaknesses:

1. As demonstrated by Brickell (1974), multi-stage sampling, if done by nomination rather than random selection at each

stage, could result in a greater degree of statistical bias as the sampling proceeded from one stage to the next.

2. Self-report questions on language and ethnicity in survey research are notorious for their difficulties in collecting accurate data (DeVries, 1985). Lack of salience of ethnicity in a multilingual context and lack of correspondence between measures of ethnic membership render the interpretation of most survey data on language and ethnicity very difficult.

3. Item nonresponses present a potential threat to the validity of a study using listwise deletion since the students who have complete data for all the variables may not be equivalent to the students for whom complete information is not available (Wolfle, 1985). Pairwise deletion can reduce the threat to some degree but may not eliminate it completely.

Chapter Two

Methodology

The High School and Beyond Data Set

Multi-Wave, Multi-Cohort Design

The data used in this study came from a subset of the 1980 High School and Beyond (HSB) database—the first wave of a national longitudinal study of high school sophomore and senior cohorts in the United States. Funded by the National Center for Education Statistics (NCES) and conducted by the National Opinion Research Center (NORC), the HSB database includes the data files for the Base Year (1980) through First Follow-up (1982), Second Follow-up (1984), and Third Follow-up (1986), with the Fourth Follow-up (1988) being scheduled.

Since this study only made use of the 1980 Base Year data, the following descriptions of the HSB data set will be limited to the Base Year exclusively.

Sampling Procedure

The HSB Base Year design included a stratified national probability sample of over 58, 200 high school students enrolled in 1,015 public and private high schools across the nation. The sampling procedure involved a two-stage stratified selection: First, 1,015 high schools were selected within a stratum drawn with a probability proportional to school size. Then, within each school up to 36 sophomores and 36 seniors were drawn again with a probability proportional to class size.

Of special interest is the weighting system used in the HSB data set. Weights were calculated and assigned to each student in the sample to reflect the over-sampling of some language minority groups (Hispanics) and some special types of schools (e.g., public alternative, Catholic with high black population)

(NORC, 1980). The design weights of the HSB study, however, were not used in this study because no group comparison was made between the pooled language minority group and the Anglo group.

HSB Data Files

With the aim of observing the educational and occupational plans and activities of American young adults passing through the post-secondary educational system, the HSB data set provides a rich source of data from students, their parents, their teachers, their friends, and school administrators. A total of some 1,900 variables were included in eight data files—Student File, Language File, School File, Teacher Comment File, Parent File, Twin/Sibling File, and Friend File. (See Appendix A for a brief description of each of the eight HSB data files.) Table 2 summarizes the file structure of the Base Year HSB data set.

This study uses two of the eight data files—the Student File, from which the social, familial, psychological and achievement variables were drawn; and the Language File, from which the ethnic language background variables were drawn.

Subjects

Identification of Ethnicity

If a student indicated a non-English language in response to any or all of five language questions in the Student Identification Pages (see Appendix B, Questions 11-15), he or she was then asked to complete the following set of questions concerning childhood language experiences, formal and informal learning of the ethnic language, patterns of other ethnic language usage, etc. Such information was collected in the Language File and the student was coded as having language data available and was identified as a language minority.

Ethnicity was further identified by two other items on the Student File: One asked "What is your race?" A total of six races were coded representing Black, White, American Indian, Asian, and Other. The other item asked: "What is your origin or descent?" A total of 30 origins were coded representing different countries or regions in the world.

Table 2
File Structure of Base Year HSB Data Set

Data File Name	Number of Cases	Number of Variables
Student File	58,270	638
Language File	11,303	42
School File	988	237
Teacher Comment File	27,786	30
Parent File	7,200	307
Test File	53,000	248
Twin/Sibling File	2,718	640
Friend File	36,000	4

Note. Adapted from "The High School and Beyond Data Set: Its Relevance for Bilingual Education Research" by A. Y. So, 1983, *NABE Journal*, 7(3), 13-21.

Using the above three pieces of information, three ethnic groups were identified.

Anglo. If a student had no language data available and indicated "White" in response to the race question, he or she was identified as a language majority student belonging to the "Anglo" ethnic group. European students with non-English language as primary language were excluded from this group.

Hispanic. If a student had language data available and indicated "Hispanic" or "Spanish" in response to the origin question, he or she was identified as a language minority student belonging to the "Hispanic" ethnic group. As such, the Hispanic group included both recent immigrants and second and third generations of early immigrants.

Asian. If a student had language data available and indicated "Asian" in response to the race question, he or she was identified as a language minority student belonging to the "Asian" ethnic group. Again, the Asian group as defined here included both recent immigrants and second and third generations of early immigrants.

Unbalanced Multi-Group Design

Before an appropriate sample size could be determined, several preliminary decisions had to be made:

1. Public schools or private schools? Because of the well-documented school-related effects (Keith & Page, 1985; Lomax, 1985), it was decided to include only public school students in this study to control for probable school effect.

2. Sophomores or seniors? Because several cognitive tests (e.g., writing and science) were available only for the sophomore students, it was decided to include only sophomores in this study to collect as much information on achievement as possible.

3. Pairwise or listwise deletion? Because one statistical assumption for the chi-square test in LISREL is that there be no missing data (Dillon & Goldstein, 1984) and because both listwise and pairwise deletion methods have been empirically demonstrated to cause no biased conclusions (Lomax, 1985), it was decided that listwise deletion was preferred over pairwise deletion.

4. Balanced or unbalanced design? To avoid the problems involved in comparing significance test results across groups of vastly disproportionate sample sizes (Wang, 1986), a balanced design with equal group sizes was preferred over stratified probability sampling. Furthermore, studies have shown that a group size of 200 is appropriate for its optimal statistical power for a chi-square test for model-data fit (Cohen, 1977) and relative robustness to minor model misspecification (Boomsma, 1982).

In practice, however, a balanced design with a group size of 200 was not feasible. Since it was anticipated that Asian students comprised the smallest proportion of the total population, all Asian students in the data set satisfying the first three criteria (public sophomore students with no missing data on the eighteen variables) were identified; there were only 117 of them. To use a balanced design as was originally planned would have meant to randomly sample 117 qualified cases from each of the Hispanic and Anglo-groups—a practice that risked too high a sampling error for the Hispanic and Anglo populations.

Based on the above theoretical and practical considerations, an unbalanced multi-group design in which the group sizes differed by no more than a factor of 3 to 3.5 was adopted. The final group sizes were 117 for the Asian, 248 for the Hispanic, and 374 for the Anglo.

Variables

The procedure for operationalizing the eighteen indicator variables used in this study is described in this section. A total of some 50 survey items were considered for use in constructing those indicator variables; among them some were factor analyzed to determine their clustering and eligibility for inclusion in forming the indicator variables. See the section on Analyses in this chapter for further information on the factor analysis procedure.

Ethnic-Language Dominance

1. *ELCHILD (use of ethnic language as a child).* This variable was constructed from the following two survey items: (a) "What was the first language you spoke when you were a child?" and (b) "What *other* language did you speak when you were a child—before you started school?"

   The variable ELCHILD was coded as follows to indicate the degree of monolingualism during childhood: 1—mono-English (if the student answered English to the first question, and None or English to the second); 2—bilingual or multilingual (if the student answered any non-English to the first question and English to the second); 3—mono-ethnic language (if the student answered any non-English to both questions). Thus, the higher the value of ELCHILD, the more frequent use of the ethnic language during childhood.

2. *CURREL (current use of ethnic language).* This variable was constructed from the following ten survey items: (a) "How often do you speak the ethnic language to your mother?" (b) "How often does your mother speak the ethnic language to you?" (c) "How often do you speak the ethnic language to your father?" (d) "How often does your father speak the ethnic language to you?" (e) "How often do your parents speak that language to each other?" (f) "How often do other relatives speak that language around you?" (g) "How often do you speak that language with your best friends?" (h) "How often do you speak that language in school with other students?" (i) "How often do you speak that language in the stores you go to?" and (j) "How often do you speak that language at work?"

   The response to the above ten items were coded as: 1—Always or almost; 2—Mostly; 3—About half; 4—Sometimes; 5—Never. The scale was then reversed and the responses were summed to form the CURREL variable. Thus the possible values of CURREL range from 10 to 50. High values of CURREL indicate high frequency of the use of ethnic language at the time of the survey.

3. *YRSUS (Years of residence in the U.S.).* The variable YRSUS was constructed from the three survey items: (a) "How much of his life has your father spent in the U.S.?" (b) "How much of her life has your mother spent in the U.S.?" and (c) "How much of your life have you spent in the U.S.?"

   The values to the first two questions were coded as: 1—all or almost all; 2—more than 20 years but not all; 3—about 11-20 years; 4—about 6-10 years; 5—about 1-5 years. The values for the third question were coded as follows: 1—All or almost all; 2—More than 10 years but not all; 3—About 6-10 years; 4—About 1-5 years. The scales were first reversed and then the three items were summed. Thus, the possible values of YRSUS range from -14 to -3. Higher values of YRSUS indicate longer period of residence in the U.S.

As one of the four indicator variables for ethnic-language dominance, however, the scale of YRSUS was again reversed by taking the negative value of YRSUS in accordance with the theoretical assumption that the longer the years of residence in the U.S., the less likely that a language minority student is ethnic language dominant.

4. *ELABL (ethnic language ability)*. This variable was constructed from the following four items: (a) "How well do you understand your ethnic language when people speak it?" (b) "How well do you speak that language?" (c) "How well do you read that language?" (d) "How well do you write that language?" Responses to the above four items were coded as: 1—very well; 2—pretty well; 3—not very well; 4—not at all. The scale was then reversed and the responses were summed to form the variable ELABL. Thus the possible values of ELABL fall in the range of 4 and 16. The higher the value of ELABL, the more proficient the student was in his or her ethnic language.

Socio-Economic Status

The HSB data set provides some twelve survey items that ask about parents' education and occupation, family income, and household possessions such as encyclopedia, typewriter, dishwasher, etc. These items were recoded using the recoding scheme suggested by Lomax (1985) as follows.

5. *PAROCC (parental occupation)*. The responses to the questions about parents' occupation were first recoded as follows: clerical = 43.5; craftsman = 36.4; farmer = 44; homemaker = 41.0; laborer = 21.5; military = 49.5; manager/administrator = 53.5; operative = 32.4; professional I = 56.5; professional II = 72.8; proprietor = 48.3; protective service = 44.8; sales = 42.3; school teacher = 60.5; service = 29.2; technical = 52.0; not working = 41.0. These recoded values were computed by taking the mean over job titles within each occupational category, using the U.S. ratings of Standard Index of Occupational Prestige (Lomax,

1985). The two items were then summed to form the PAROCC variable; thus high values of PAROCC indicate high status of father's and mother's occupation.

6. *PARED (parental education)*. The responses to the questions about parents' education were first recoded as follows: below high school = 11; high school graduate = 12; post-high school and less than two years schooling = 13; post-high school and two years schooling = 14; college graduate = 16; master's degree = 18; professional degree = 19. The two items were then summed to form the PARED variable; thus the higher the PARED value, the higher the father's and mother's education.

7. *INCOME (family income)*. The variable INCOME was constructed from the single item which asked about the family' annual income. The responses were recoded as follows: below \$7,000 = 3.5; \$7-12,000 = 9.5; \$12-16,000 = 14; \$16-20,000 = 18; \$20-25,000 = 22.5; \$25-38,000 = 31.5; over \$38,000 = 45.

8. *POSSESS (household possessions)*. Several items on the HSB survey were designed to be indicative of household possessions: study place, newspaper, encyclopedia, typewriter, dishwasher, two or more cars, 50 or more books, own room, calculator.

    Responses to these items were coded as 1—yes; 2—no. They were first recoded as 1 = yes and 0 = no; then they were summed to form the composite POSSESS. The possible value of POSSESS range from 0 to 9. The higher the POSSESS, the more the household possessions.

Parental Involvement

9. *PARSCHL (parental involvement in school work)*. This variable was constructed from the following two items: (a) "Does your mother keep close track of how well you are doing in school?" (b) "Does your father keep close track of how well you are doing in school?"

The responses to the above two items were coded as follows: 1—true; 2—false. The scale was first reversed and then the responses were summed to form the variable PARSCHL. The possible values of PARSCHL range from 2 to 4. High values of PARSCHL indicate high level of parental involvement.

10. *PARPLAN (parental involvement in study plan)*. This variable was constructed from the following two items: (a) "How much have you talked to your father about planning your school program?" and (b) "How much have you talked to your mother about planning your school program?"

The variable PARPLAN was the sum of the responses to the above two items coded as follows: 1—not at all; 2—somewhat; 3—a great deal. The possible values of PARPLAN fall in the range of 2 to 6. Again, high values of PARPLAN indicate high level of parental involvement.

Psychological Orientation

11. *CONCPT (self-concept)*. There were six items initially considered for forming the variable CONCPT; (a) "I take a positive attitude toward myself," (b) "I am a person of worth on an equal plane with others," (c) "I am able to do things as well as most other people," (d) "on the whole, I am satisfied with myself," (e) "At times I think I am no good at all," and (f) "I feel I do not have much to be proud of."

Responses to the above items were originally coded as follows: 1—strongly agree; 2—agree; 3—disagree; 4—strongly disagree. The scales for the first four items were reversed and all six were subjected to an exploratory factor analysis. The results indicated that only the first three items were consistent measures of self-concept and therefore the responses to the three items were summed to form the variable CONCPT. Thus the possible values of CONCPT range from 3 to 12. High values of CONCPT indicate high level of self-concept.

12. *CONTRL (internal locus of control)*. The six items initially considered for measuring internal locus of control were: (a) "Good luck is more important than hard work for success," (b) "Planning only makes a person unhappy, since plans hardly ever work out anyway," (c) "People who accept their condition in life are happier than those who try to change things," (d) "Every time I try to get ahead, something or somebody stops me," (e) "What happens to me is my own doing," and (f) "When I make plans, I am almost certain I can make them work."

Responses were originally coded the same way as the self-concept items. The scales for the last two items were reversed and all six items were subjected to an exploratory factor analysis. The results indicated that only the first three items were consistent measures of internal locus of control; therefore these three items were summed to form the variable CONTRL. The possible values of CONTRL range from 3 to 12. Again, high values of CONTRL indicate high level of internal locus of control.

13. *MOT (motivation)*. Initially seven survey items were considered for forming the variable MOT: (a) "I am satisfied with the way my education is going." (b) "I like to work hard in school," (c) "I am interested in school," (d) "Math is useful in my future," (e) "Math is interesting to me." (f) "English is useful in my future," and (g) "English is interesting to me."

Responses were originally coded as 1 representing Yes, and 2 representing No. They were recoded as 1 = yes and 0 = no. Exploratory factor analysis indicated that only (a) and (b) were consistently measures of motivation across all three ethnic groups; thus the other items were dropped from further analysis. The variable MOT was simply the sum of the two remaining items, with the possible values ranging from 0 to 2. High MOT values represent high motivation.

Verbal Achievement

14. *VOCAB (vocabulary score).* This variable was the number-right score on a 21-item, 7-minute vocabulary test administered at the time of the survey. The vocabulary test used synonym format to test the knowledge of vocabulary.

15. *READING (reading score).* This variable was the number-right score on a 20-item, 15-minute reading test administered at the time of the survey. The reading test consisted of short passages (100-200 words) with several related questions concerning a variety of reading skills (analysis and interpretation) but focusing on straight-forward comprehension.

16. *WRITING (writing score).* This variable was the number-right score on a 17-item, 10-minute writing test administered at the time of the survey. The writing test was designed to test writing ability and knowledge of basic grammar.

Quantitative Achievement

17. *MATH (math score).* This variable was the number-right score on two math tests: part I was a 28-item, 16-minute test and part II was a 10-item, 5-minute test, both administered at the time of the survey. The test was composed of quantitative comparisons in which the student indicated which of two quantities was greater, or equal, or asserted their inequality for the lack of sufficient data.

18. *SCIENCE (science score).* This variable was the number-right score on a 20-item, 10-minute science test administered at the time of the survey. The science test was designed to test science knowledge and scientific reasoning ability.

Notes on Variable Scaling
The majority of the indicator variables were linear composites of a number of survey items with equal weight for each item.

While the use of factor weights (as done in Page and Keith's 1981 study for the ability variable) may have been more desirable in reducing measurement error, LISREL modeling separated the measurement error from the common variance. Therefore a linear equal-weighting scheme was used in recoding the relevant survey items.

Another concern was the requirement for interval data in LISREL models since the majority of the indicator variables (13 out of 18) were ordinal rather than interval. Fortunately it has been demonstrated that if the number of categories is four or greater and the skewness does not exceed 2.0 in absolute value, then the resultant estimates will not be unduly biased (Muthen, 1982, cited in Lomax, 1985, p. 218). Since most of the ordinal variables (11 out of 13) had four or more categories, the requirement for interval data was deemed irrelevant. If, however, these variables turned out to be highly skewed, then special control cards should be used in the LISREL programs to request polychoric or polyserial correlations be analyzed rather than ordinary product moment correlations (Jöreskog & Sörbom, 1984, p. IV.3). In addition, unweighed least-square (ULS) estimation would be preferred over maximum-likelihood (ML) estimation since the correlation matrix might not be positive definite (Jöreskog & Sörbom, 1984, p. IV.6).

Procedure

Given the nature of secondary data analysis, detailed treatment of the procedure of data manipulation is often deemed desirable. The preceding sections already touched on this topic to some extent. This section will describe in more detail the temporal steps involved in arriving at the final analyses of interest. (See Figure 1 for a flowchart diagram illustrating the following steps.)

Step 1: Identifying HSB Data Files
Out of the eight data files currently available for the HSB Base Year data set, only two contain the variables of interest: the Student File and the Language File. These two files were pur-

Figure 1. Procedure of variable selection from Base Year HSB data set.

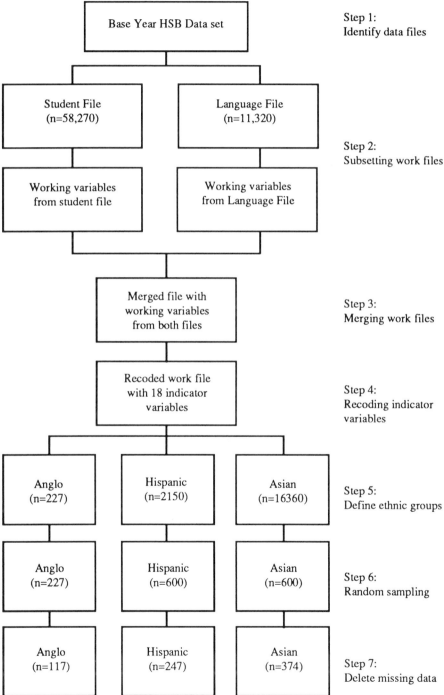

chased from the National Center for Education Statistics on two IBM standard labelled tapes.

Step 2: Subsetting Work Files
The next step was to select the variables of interest on the tapes. A simple frequency analysis on the discrete variables (e.g., origin, SES) and a descriptive analysis on the continuous variables (e.g., CONCPT, MATH) helped confirm the reading of tape positions.

Step 3: Merging Work Files
After all the relevant variables had been identified, they were then merged by the student ID's (variable name CASEID) and output onto a blank tape for permanent storage. The large number of observations made using disks as the storage device infeasible. All subsequent analyses were performed on this merged data file to preserve the integrity of the original HSB data files.

Step 4: Creating Indicator Variables
The eighteen indicator variables were then created from the selected working variables in the work files and then recoded to the scales as described in the previous section.

Step 5: Defining Ethnic Groups
The next step was to define the three ethnic groups as described before. Three items in the Student File (language data, race, and origin) were used for coding ethnicity. Two other questions were used for further qualifying the eligible sample: school type (public school only) and grade level (sophomore only).

Step 6: Random Sampling by Group
After the three ethnic groups had been defined as above, only 227 Asian students remained as eligible sample, compared to 2,150 Hispanics and 16,360 Anglos. 600 students were then randomly selected from the Hispanic and Anglo groups respectively in anticipation of losing one-third to one-half of the data in each group as a result of missing data.

The random samples were selected by using the random number generator function in SAS and by using the exact-size, random-sampling-without-replacement procedure (SAS Institute, 1987, pp. 227-229).

Step 7: Deleting Missing Data
The last step was to delete from the total eligible sample all the cases with non-response to any of the eighteen indicator variables. This practice further reduced the group sizes to 117 in the Asian group, 248 in the Hispanic, and 374 in the Anglo.

By this stage, the data collection procedure was completed.

Analyses

Statistical Software
The Statistical Analysis System (SAS) package (SAS Institute, 1985a and b) was used to create the unbalanced multi-group sample, compute descriptive statistics of the indicator variables, and perform exploratory factor analysis on the psychological orientation variables. For linear structural relations analysis, the LISREL package installed as part of the Statistical Package for Social Sciences (SPSSx) software was used, which could accommodate confirmatory factor analysis as well as covariance structure analysis (Jöreskog & Sörbom, 1984). Both software packages were installed on the IBM Virtual Machine (VM) 4341/4381 model under the Conversational Monitor System (CMS) operating system (IBM Corporation, 1983).

LISREL Terms and Notation
A LISREL model is a covariance structure model consisting of either or both of the two components: a measurement model and a structural-equation model. The measurement model specifies how the latent construct is measured in terms of the observed variables and is used to describe the measurement properties (reliabilities and validities) of the observed variables. The structural-equation model relates the latent constructs in a hypothesized causal network and is used to describe the causal effects and the amount of unexplained variance (Jöreskog & Sörbom, 1984, p. I.3).

The notation in the causal models in this study followed the conventions used in most LISREL studies. Latent exogenous variables are denoted by ξ (ksi) and latent endogenous variables by η (eta). Observed exogenous variables are denoted by X and observed endogenous variables by Y. Effects of latent exogenous variables on latent endogenous variables are denoted by γ (gamma) and latent endogenous variables on latent endogenous variables by β (beta). The factor loading relating each observed variable to its latent construct is denoted by λ (lambda). The error term for each structural equation relating a set of exogenous and endogenous explanatory variables to an endogenous criterion variable is denoted by ζ (zeta). Errors in the measurement of the observed exogenous variables are denoted by δ (delta) and error in the measurement of the observed endogenous variables by ε (epsilon). All matrices of the LISREL parameters are denoted by their corresponding capital Greek letters.

In drawing LISREL diagrams, all observed variables are represented by squares, all unobserved variables by circles. The correlation between two latent exogenous variables is denoted by ϕ (phi) and the correlation between two disturbance errors by ψ (psi); both are depicted by curved lines with double-headed arrows. All paths, in the form of uni-directional arrows, are drawn from the variables taken as causes to the variables taken as effects. Each path coefficient is referenced by two subscripts: the first being the variable taken as the effect, the second being the variable taken as the cause. All loadings and errors are referenced by a single subscript. Alternatively, each parameter can be referenced by its coordinates in the parameter matrix, e.g., BE(4,2), indicating the element in the fourth row and second column of the BETA matrix. The column position indicates the cause and the row position indicates the effect.

In algebraic terms, a LISREL model can be described by the following three mathematical equations (Jöreskog and Sörbom, 1984, p. I.6):

(i) Structural Equation Model: $\eta = B\eta + \Gamma\xi + \zeta$

(ii) Measurement Model for Y: $Y = \Lambda_y\eta + \varepsilon$

(iii) Measurement Model for X: $X = \Lambda_x \xi + \delta$

with the assumptions:

(i) ζ is uncorrelated with ξ

(ii) ε is uncorrelated with η

(iii) δ is uncorrelated with ξ

(iv) ζ, ε, and δ are mutually uncorrelated when in deviation-score form; and

(v) B has zeroes in the diagonal and I - B is non-singular.

Sample-Population Invariance

The procedure of arriving at the three ethnic groups at various sampling stages is summarized in Table 3.

Initially (stage I) there were 714 Asian, 6,698 Hispanic, and 43,854 Anglo students. After eliminating non-public school sophomores and all seniors (stage II), 269 Asian, 2,975 Hispanic, and 18,200 Anglo students remained. Upon further qualifying ethnicity with the availability of language data (stage III), 227 Asian, 2,150 Hispanic, and 16,360 Anglo students were left. From the Hispanic and Anglo groups, 600 students were then randomly selected from each group (stage IV). Finally, after excluding all the students who failed to respond to one or more of the 18 indicator variables (stage V), only 117 Asian, 248 Hispanic, and 374 Anglo students were retained for further analysis.

When moving from stage III to stage IV, a random sample was selected from its "population" (which was in fact a sample of its "population" at the preceding stage) for the Anglo and Hispanic students respectively. Some measure must be taken to ensure that the random sample was statistically comparable to its population. Although a multivariate significance test which tests the equivalence of two population centroids would be preferred over separate univariate single-sample z-tests which test the equivalence of a sample mean to its population mean, the large number of survey items involved rendered it a formidable

Table 3
Group Sizes at Various Sampling Stages

	Sampling Stage				
	I	II	III	IV	V
Group	Original	Public sch. sophomore	Language data	Random sample	Non-missing
Asian	714	269	227	227	117
Hispanic	6,698	2,975	2,150	600	248
Anglo	43,854	18,200	16,360	600	374
Total	51,266	21,444	18,737	1,427	739

task.   As a result, a series of single-sample two-tailed z-tests comparing the stage III sample with the stage IV sample on some 35 items were performed for the Hispanic and Anglo groups separately.

Exploratory Factor Analysis
Nineteen survey items presumably measuring psychological orientation were factor analyzed to examine how they clustered to form the three indicator variables: self-concept, internal locus of control, and motivation. Instead of subjecting the nineteen items to factor analysis in a purely exploratory fashion, the number of factors to be retained was fixed at three—self-concept, internal locus of control, and motivation, regardless of the magnitudes of the eigenvalues associated with the factors. Items with non-meaningful loadings (less than .3) and items loading on multiple factors (i.e., complex variables) were dropped from further analysis.

The principal axis factoring method was used with squared multiple correlations (SMC) as the initial communality estimates on the diagonal of the correlation matrix to be factored (Harman, 1976).   Both iterative and non-iterative procedures were performed for purposes of comparison.   An orthogonal factor solution using a varimax rotation (Kaiser, 1958) was followed by an oblique factor solution using a promax rotation (SAS Institute, 1985b).

Univariate Statistics

After the measurement components of the LISREL model had been empirically specified, preliminary analysis of the indicator variables followed. Univariate statistics—means, standard deviations, skewness, and kurtosis—of the indicator variables were computed and the variance-covariance matrix as well as the correlation matrix of the indicator variables were calculated as the input for subsequent LISREL runs.

Of particular concern was the assumption of multivariate normality in LISREL analysis. When the maximum likelihood method is used for parameter estimation, the statistical theory on which the LISREL model is based requires that the indicator variables come from a multivariate normal distribution.

However, it has been proven difficult to construct a "good" overall test of joint normality in more than two dimensions (Johnson & Wichern, 1982). Moreover, when the N is large enough, the central limit theorem tells us that the sampling distribution of the sample mean is always nearly normal whatever the form of the underlying parent population (see Johnson & Wichern, 1982, pp. 148-149 for proof). Since the sample in this study was large enough for the central limit theorem to apply and the data space was 18-dimensional, a formal test of multivariate normal distribution was judged neither feasible nor essential for this study.

Glimpses of multivariate normality, however, could be gained from a check on univariate normality of the marginals. It has been shown that for most practical work, univariate and bivariate investigations are usually sufficient since data that are normal in lower-dimensional representations but non-normal in higher dimensions have not been detected frequently. Univariate tests of normality also provide some empirical ground for the use of ordinal data where interval data are assumed. When a univariate distribution turned out to deviate severely from normality, the variable would be transformed by recoding and regrouping some of the extreme categories so that more nearly normally distributed data could be obtained.

In addition to the above simple statistics, zero-order correlations among the indicator variables were also calculated as a routine part of reporting. Generalized variances of the sets of correlation coefficients were examined which assessed the "ill-conditioning" of the correlation matrices (see the section on Preliminary Analyses in Chapter Three).

Confirmatory Factor Analysis

Confirmatory factor analysis was used to evaluate the measurement models of the exogenous variables and endogenous variables separately (see Figure 2). This analysis provides the following information for evaluating the measurement models (see Dillon & Goldstein, 1984, pp. 479-485): (a) the reliability of each indicator variable determined by the squared multiple correlation for each indicator variable with the other variables in the model; (b) a reliability estimate of each measurement model, determined by the coefficient of determination; and (c) the validity of each measurement model determined by the shared variance or the ratio of the variance captured by the construct over that variance plus the variance due to measurement error.

Single-Group Analysis

After the adequacy of the two measurement models had been evaluated, they were linked together to form the full covariance structure models (see Figure 3 for the initial covariance structure model for the language minority group and Figure 4 for the language majority group). The difference between Figure 3 and Figure 4 was the elimination of ethnic-language dominance from the language majority model for the obvious reason—no ethnic language data was applicable to the language majority students. In addition, no path was postulated from verbal achievement to quantitative achievement for the language majority group.

The causal paths in both models were suggested by the literature review in Chapter One. For example, ethnic-language dominance was hypothesized to affect English verbal achievement, which in turn influenced quantitative achievement. However, for lack of convincing and conclusive theoretical support, the causal linkage was not expected to be strong.

Figure 2. Initial measurement models for exogenous and endogenous variables.

Exogenous Variables

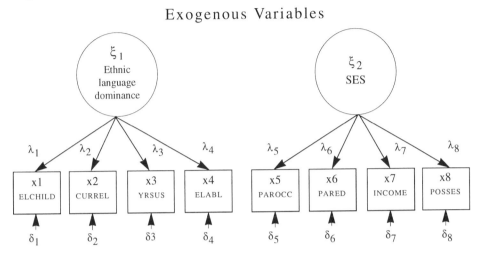

Endogenous Variables

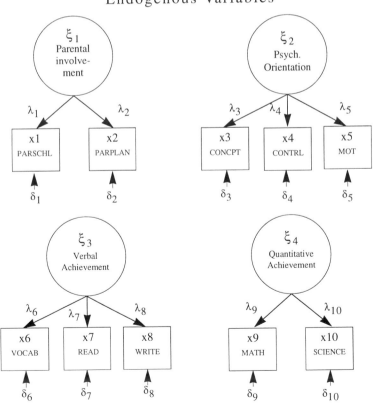

Figure 3. Initial structural covariance model for language minority groups (Asian & Hispanic).

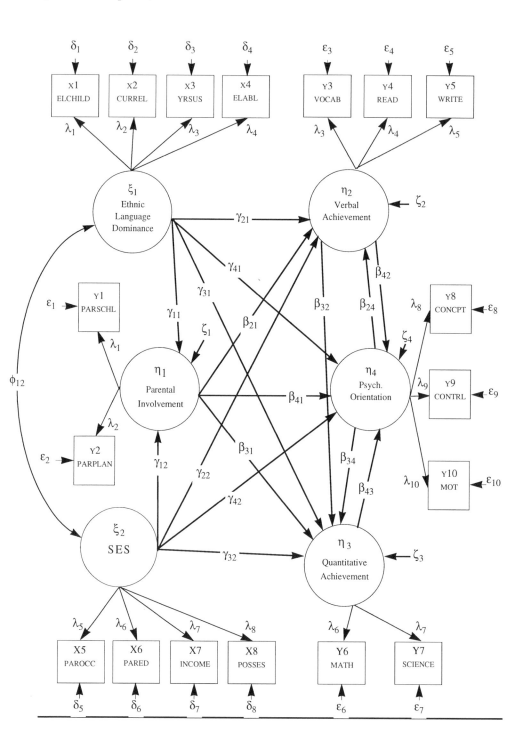

Figure 4. Initial structural covariance model for language majority group (Anglo).

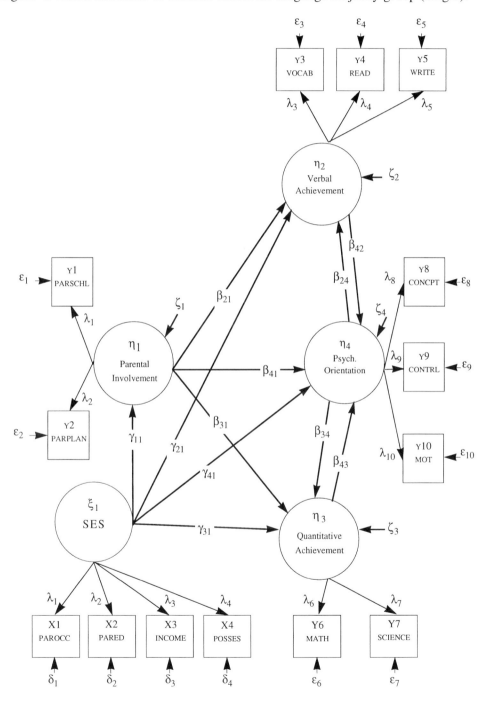

Similarly, the causality between psychological orientation and achievement was assumed to be reciprocal, but evidence was lacking in the relative strengths of the directions.

As a result of lacking strong theoretical support, the initial models were "saturated" models in that few restrictions were placed on the possible causal paths among the constructs. This posed the identifiability problem of the models, as discussed in the last section of this chapter.

The adequacy of the initial models was then evaluated by the chi-square test, the chi-square/df ratio, the goodness-of-fit index, normalized residuals, and root mean-square residual. Significance of path coefficients and magnitudes of modification indices were then used for guiding the specification search for better-fitting models. Each modification was evaluated by both its theoretical plausibility and its resultant chi-square difference. This procedure was repeated until an optimally-fitting model was found for each ethnic group.

Multi-Group Analysis
To test whether a generic covariance structure model held for the two language minority groups (Hispanic and Asian) and between each of the two language minority groups and the language majority group (Anglo), the invariance of the factor structures was tested by simultaneously estimating the parameters for the two groups of interest. Equality constraints were imposed in the simultaneous model in a hierarchical order as follows: (a) invariance of factor loadings, (b) invariance of factor loadings and measurement errors, (c) invariance of factor loadings, measurement errors, and variances and covariances of the factors; and (d) invariance of the variance-covariance matrices.

Provided that the measurement models were found to be invariant, the test on the invariance of the structural-equation models would then follow. Any given single structural parameter or matrix could be set to be invariant, and the chi-square difference could be tested for significant deterioration in goodness-of-fit.

For the comparison between each of the language minority groups and the language majority group, it was hypothesized that after the ethnic-language dominance construct was deleted from the model, the optimal-fitting model for the Anglo group was more invariant between the Asian and the Anglo than between the Hispanic and the Anglo. The relative degree of invariance was judged by the expected better model-data fit in the comparison between the Asian and the Anglo than between the Hispanic and the Anglo.

Pooled-Sample Analysis
Lastly, the two language minority groups were combined to form a pooled minority sample for testing the ethnicity effect (see Figure 5 for the pooled-sample covariance structure model). Ethnicity (or group membership) was dichotomously coded into the model, with 1 representing the Asians and 0 the Hispanics. This practice allowed for testing the net effects of the hypothesized causal factors on school outcomes after partialing out ethnicity.

With ethnicity being a dichotomous variable, the LISREL control card "MV = 2" was added in the program to designate the dichotomy of the variable.

The above practice of pooled-sample analysis, however, was based on the assumption that the two language minority groups were invariant. If it turned out that from the multi-group analysis the two groups were not invariant, then pooling would not be justified. Interpretation of the causal network would then be based on the single-group analysis rather than the pooled-sample analysis.

Model Identification
Before parameter estimation can proceed, identification of the covariance structure model must be demonstrated. The identification problem seeks to answer the question: Is there a unique set of parameter values consistent with the data? If not, the model may be underidentified and only some of the parameters can be estimated.

A number of criteria have been proposed for examining the identifiability of a structural equation and a covariance structure model. They are discussed below.

Figure 5. Initial structural covariance model for pooled language minority sample.

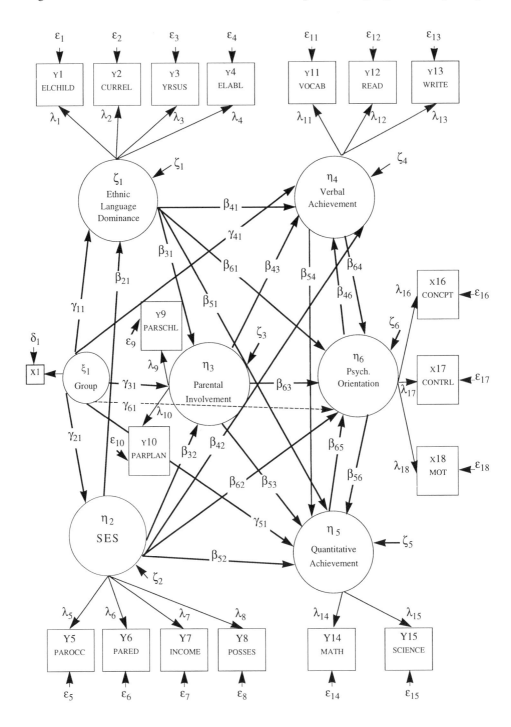

Identification of covariance structure models. A necessary but not sufficient condition for model identification is that the number of independent parameters being estimated is less than or equal to the number of non-redundant elements of the sample variance-covariance matrix (Long, 1983b). That is, let t be the total number of independent parameters in a covariance structure model, n be the total of X and Y variables, and s be the number of non-redundant elements in the sample variance-covariance matrix, then a necessary condition for identification of all the parameters in the model is

$$t <= s,$$

where $s = (n)(n + 1) / 2$.

In the initial single-group covariance structure model for the language minority groups, there were eighteen X and Y indicator variables; thus,

$$n = 18$$
$$s = 18\,(18 + 1)/2 = 171$$
$$t = 8\ \Lambda x\text{'s} + 10\ \Lambda y\text{'s} + 8\ \delta\text{'s} + 10\ \varepsilon\text{'s} + 3\ \phi\text{'s} + 8\ \gamma\text{'s} + 8\ \beta\text{'s} +$$
$$4\ \zeta\text{'s} = 59;$$

therefore, t (59) is less than s (171); the necessary condition for the language minority model is satisfied. Similar operation shows that the necessary condition for the language majority model is also satisfied.

Another necessary but still not sufficient condition for model identification involves the information matrix, i.e., the probability limit of the matrix of second-order derivatives of the fitting function used to estimate the model (Jöreskog & Sörbom, 1984, p. I.24), or less technically, the matrix of variances and covariances of the parameter estimates (Kmenta, 1971, pp. 174-186). It has been demonstrated that for a model to be identified, the information matrix must be positive definite (Jöreskog, 1978).

To demonstrate the positive definiteness of an information matrix, Jöreskog & Sörbom, (1984, p. I.24) suggest that different sets of starting values be used as input to the ML estimation procedure to see if consistent estimates result. If so, then the information matrix is positive definite.

A necessary and sufficient condition for model identification is to prove mathematically that the parameters can be solved for in terms of the variances and covariances of the observed variables. This can be achieved by first demonstrating that the measurement components of the LISREL model are identified, including the variances and covariances of the factors. Then the structural parameters can be identified by solving for them in terms of the covariances among the factors (Long, 1983b).

Unfortunately, the mathematical proof for the above necessary and sufficient condition can be very difficult to carry out. As an alternative, researchers often turn to the positive definiteness of the information matrix for proof of identification. If the information matrix is positive definite, then it is almost certain that the model is identified.

Identification of structural equations. A necessary condition for a structural equation to be identified is that the number of exogenous variables excluded from the equation be at least as great as one less than the number of endogenous variables included in the equation (Jöreskog & Sörbom, 1984, p. III.44). Another way to describe this condition is that, in terms of the constraints on the beta matrix and the gamma matrix, the number of coefficients fixed to zero in a given row of the beta matrix and the gamma matrix be greater than or equal to the number of equations minus one (Long, 1983b). This is called the "order condition" for the identification of a structural equation.

Table 4 summarizes the above two alternative ways of checking the order conditions of the four structural equations in the single-group covariance structure model for the language minority groups. The four structural equations are as follows:

$$\text{Eq. 1: } \eta_1 = 0\eta_1 + 0\eta_2 + 0\eta_3 + 0\eta_4 + \gamma_{11}\xi_1 + \gamma_{12}\xi_2 + \zeta_1$$
$$\text{Eq. 2: } \eta_2 = \beta_{21}\eta_1 + 0\eta_2 + 0\eta_3 + \beta_{24}\eta_4 + \gamma_{21}\xi_1 + \gamma_{22}\xi_2 + \zeta_2$$
$$\text{Eq. 3: } \eta_3 = \beta_{31}\eta_1 + \beta_{32}\eta_2 + 0\eta_3 + \beta_{34}\eta_4 + \gamma_{31}\xi_1 + \gamma_{32}\xi_2 + \zeta_3$$
$$\text{Eq. 4: } \eta_4 = \beta_{41}\eta_1 + \beta_{42}\eta_2 + \beta_{43}\eta_3 + 0\eta_4 + \gamma_{41}\xi_1 + \gamma_{42}\xi_2 + \zeta_4$$

It is clear that both methods point to the same conclusion that only the first structural equation satisfies the order condition.

Table 4
Order Conditions for Structural Equations in Single-Group Covariance Structure Model

Eq.	Number of excl. exog. var.	> = ?	Number of incl. endg. var. -1	Identification
1	0	Yes	-1	Yes
2	0	No	1	No
3	0	No	2	No
4	0	No	2	No

Eq.	Number of coeff. fixed to zero	> = ?	Number of equations -1	Identification
1	4	Yes	3	Yes
2	2	No	3	No
3	1	No	3	No
4	1	No	3	No

A necessary *and* sufficient condition for an equation to be identified is described by Long (1983b): Let $\underline{B}^{\#}$ be the matrix formed by excluding the row of $[\underline{I} - \underline{B}]$ for the equation being considered, and deleting all columns for which there is not a zero in the excluded row. Let $\Gamma^{\#}$ be the matrix formed by the same operation on the gamma matrix. An equation is identified if and only if the rank of $[\underline{B}^{\#} \mid \Gamma^{\#}]$ equals the number of equations minus one. This condition is commonly termed the "rank condition."

Turning to the initial saturated covariance structure model for the language minority groups (see Figure 3), one can easily see that it is underidentified. Specifically, the mathematical equation for the structural equation model is

$$\underset{\sim}{\eta} = \underset{\sim\sim}{B\eta} + \underset{\sim\sim}{\Gamma\xi} + \underset{\sim}{\zeta}$$

In extended matrix for, this becomes

$$\begin{bmatrix} \eta_1 \\ \eta_2 \\ \eta_3 \\ \eta_4 \end{bmatrix} = \begin{bmatrix} 0 & 0 & 0 & 0 \\ \beta_{21} & 0 & 0 & \beta_{24} \\ \beta_{31} & \beta_{32} & 0 & \beta_{34} \\ \beta_{41} & \beta_{42} & \beta_{43} & 0 \end{bmatrix} \begin{bmatrix} \eta_1 \\ \eta_2 \\ \eta_3 \\ \eta_4 \end{bmatrix} + \begin{bmatrix} g_{11} g_{12} \\ \gamma_{21} \gamma_{22} \\ \gamma_{31} \gamma_{32} \\ \gamma_{41} \gamma_{42} \end{bmatrix} \begin{bmatrix} \xi_1 \\ \xi_2 \end{bmatrix} + \begin{bmatrix} \zeta_1 \\ \zeta_2 \\ \zeta_3 \\ \zeta_4 \end{bmatrix}$$

Checking against the rank condition described above, we can see that only the first structural equation satisfies the rank condition:

$$\underset{\sim}{B}_1{}^{\#} = \begin{bmatrix} \cancel{1} & \cancel{0} & \cancel{0} & \cancel{0} \\ -\beta_{21} & 1 & 0 & -\beta_{24} \\ -\beta_{31} & -\beta_{32} & 1 & -\beta_{34} \\ -\beta_{41} & -\beta_{42} & -\beta_{43} & 1 \end{bmatrix} \qquad \underset{\sim}{\Gamma}_1{}^{\#} = \begin{bmatrix} \cancel{\gamma}_{11} & \cancel{\gamma}_{12} \\ \cancel{\gamma}_{21} & \gamma_{22} \\ \cancel{\gamma}_{31} & \gamma_{32} \\ \cancel{\gamma}_{41} & \gamma_{42} \end{bmatrix}$$

$$\text{Rank} \quad [\ \underset{\sim}{B}_1{}^{\#} \mid \underset{\sim}{\Gamma}_1{}^{\#}\ ] = \begin{bmatrix} 1 & 0 & -\beta_{24} & \gamma_{22} \\ -\beta_{32} & 1 & -\beta_{34} & \gamma_{32} \\ -\beta_{42} & -\beta_{43} & 1 & \gamma_{42} \end{bmatrix} = 3$$

Therefore, the rank of the concatenated matrix equals 3, which is the number of equations (4) minus one. The first equation is thus identified. But the same operation would show that the other three equations are not identified. Similarly, the other two initial covariance structure models (see Figures 4 and 5) are also underidentified.

Several solutions were available for solving the underidentification problem of the initial saturated covariance structure models. The most preferable one would be to incorporate an instrumental variable that had no direct effect on one of the two endogenous constructs with simultaneous causality but either directly or indirectly affected the other endogenous construct. (See Heise, 1975, p. 160 for other requirements for instrumental variables). In actuality, however, it was difficult to locate such variables in the HSB data set that would, say, affect verbal achievement but not psychological orientation.

Alternatively, identification could be achieved by restricting selected elements of the beta matrix and the gamma matrix to equal zero (Wonnacott & Wonnacott, 1979, pp. 461-473). For example, by setting the paths γ_{31}, γ_{41}, γ_{22}, γ_{32} and β_{41} to zero, the model would become identified. The problem with this approach is that there was little theoretical justification for such arbitrary restriction.

As a last resort, the underidentified model could be modified by fixing some of the identified parameters to the estimated values (either zero or non-zero), thus reducing the number of parameters to be estimated in subsequent runs. It has been shown that identified parameter estimates and resulting goodness-of-fit indices are fairly invariant over model identification (Jöreskog & Sörbom, 1984, p. III.77). Unfortunately, however, non-identified parameters are still given somewhat arbitrary values.

Since there was no better solution to the identification problem of the initial covariance structure models, the decision was to take the last route and fix selected parameters in the initial underidentified models to their estimated values, thus making the models identified.

Chapter Three

Results

This chapter is divided into five major sections: (a) the preliminary analysis, which includes the comparison between the random samples and their respective HSB populations, the exploratory factor analysis on the survey items measuring psychological orientation, the simple statistics of the eighteen indicator variables, and the correlations and generalized variances; (b) the confirmatory factor analysis of the eighteen indicator variables, which provides the reliabilities of the indicator variables, and the reliabilities and validities of the optimal-fitting measurement models; (c) single-group covariance structure analysis, which estimates the structural parameters of the optimal-fitting covariance structure model for each group; (d) multi-group covariance structure analysis, which tests the invariance of the measurement models across the three ethnic groups; and lastly, (e) pooled-sample covariance structure analysis, which assesses the effect of ethnicity on the six latent constructs in the optimal-fitting covariance structure model.

Preliminary Analysis

Sample-Population Invariance

To ensure that the samples randomly selected from the eligible students in the respective ethnic populations—i.e., those sophomores in the HSB data set who were categorized as Anglo and Hispanic—were representative of their populations, a series of two-tailed single-sample z-tests were performed. The goal was to determine whether the sample means approached the population means within a reasonable range to declare that the samples did not differ significantly from the populations. A total of 35 survey items were tested individually for the sample-population equivalence. Note that this procedure was done for the Anglo and Hispanic groups only because no random sampling was performed on the Asian group as all the eligible Asian students were included in this study. The results of these single-sample z-tests are reported in Table 5.

A cursory look at this table clearly shows that the two random samples were equivalent to their respective HSB populations. Most of the z-ratios were so small that no significance tests were even necessary to justify the claim. The only minor exceptions were the "Father Monitoring School" variable for the Hispanic (z = -2.019, p = .043) and the "Math Part I" variable for the Anglo (z = 2.347, p = .019). The p-values ranged from .043 to .960, with a mean of .609 for the Hispanic, and from .019 to .968, with a mean of .513 for the Anglo. These figures suggest that the random sampling procedure used in this study was valid and unbiased.

Table 5
z-tests of Selected Survey Items for Testing
Sample-Population Invariance

Hispanic

Item	P/S	N	Mean	Sd	z	(p)
Years in US–father	P	1850	1.721	1.082	.190	(.849)
	S	522	1.730	1.080		
Years in US–mother	P	1978	1.807	1.136	-.414	(.682)
	S	554	1.787	1.114		
Years in US–self	P	2124	1.369	0.822	-.207	(.834)
	S	591	1.362	0.826		
Father's occupation	P	2150	0.592	0.491	-.100	(.920)
	S	600	0.590	0.492		
Mother's occupation	P	1564	9.497	5.572	1.132	(.258)
	S	445	9.796	5.656		
Father's education	P	1326	3.253	2.057	.953	(.342)
	S	369	3.355	2.129		
Mother's education	P	1541	3.088	1.836	-1.572	(.116)
	S	419	2.947	1.656		

Table 5 (continued)

Hispanic

Item	P/S	N	Mean	Sd	z	(p)
Income	P	1785	3.130	1.631	.123	(.904)
	S	498	3.139	0.462		
Own study place	P	1879	1.576	0.494	1.013	(.312)
	S	517	1.598	0.491		
Newspaper	P	1876	1.384	0.487	-.188	(.849)
	S	523	1.380	0.486		
Encyclopedia	P	1885	1.224	0.417	-.440	(.660)
	S	527	1.216	0.412		
Typewriter	P	1879	1.371	0.483	1.272	(.204)
	S	518	1.398	0.490		
Dishwasher	P	1834	1.772	0.420	.539	(.589)
	S	513	1.782	0.414		
Two or more cars	P	1872	1.280	0.449	.560	(.575)
	S	523	1.291	0.454		
50 or more books	P	1863	1.361	0.480	-.047	(.960)
	S	517	1.360	0.480		
Own room	P	1875	1.377	0.485	.518	(.603)
	S	521	1.388	0.488		
Calculator	P	1872	1.353	0.478	1.527	(.126)
	S	520	1.385	0.487		
Father monitor school	P	1836	1.234	0.423	-2.019	(.043)*
	S	505	1.196	0.397		
Mother monitor school	P	2041	1.118	0.322	-.591	(.555)
	S	566	1.110	0.313		
Plan program w/father	P	2008	1.863	0.718	-.198	(.841)
	S	559	1.857	0.712		
Plan program w/mother	P	2063	2.230	0.686	.105	(.912)
	S	574	2.233	0.677		
Positive attd self	P	1827	1.785	0.618	.361	(.719)
	S	498	1.795	0.620		
Person of worth	P	1820	1.809	0.608	-.221	(.826)
	S	502	1.803	0.605		
Able to do things	P	1861	1.831	0.617	.659	(.509)
	S	511	1.849	0.600		
Not pay to plan ahead	P	1855	2.788	0.817	-1.002	(.317)
	S	517	2.752	0.803		
Accept conditions	P	1747	2.309	0.806	.355	(.719)
	S	484	2.322	0.811		
Good luck not work	P	1826	2.888	0.766	-.235	(.810)
	S	508	2.880	0.743		
Interested in school	P	2002	1.167	0.373	-.316	(.749)
	S	557	1.162	0.368		

Table 5 (continued)

Hispanic

Item	P/S	N	Mean	Sd	z	(p)
Like work in school	P	1983	1.365	0.482	-.049	(.960)
	S	550	1.364	0.481		
Vocabulary	P	1835	8.494	3.823	.635	(.522)
	S	511	8.589	3.882		
Reading	P	1838	7.096	3.243	.468	(.638)
	S	514	7.163	3.354		
Writing	P	1819	8.430	3.475	-.577	(.562)
	S	508	8.341	3.375		
Math—Part I	P	1847	11.280	4.820	-.405	(.682)
	S	516	11.194	5.005		
Math—Part II	P	1825	3.501	1.692	.120	(.904)
	S	506	3.510	1.681		
Science	P	1835	8.704	3.362	-1.183	(.238)
	S	511	8.528	3.432		

Anglo

Item	P/S	N	Mean	Sd	z	(p)
Years in US—father	P	15591	1.080	0.362	.790	(.430)
	S	568	1.092	0.383		
Years in US—mother	P	15969	1.067	0.352	1.473	(.150)
	S	580	1.088	0.400		
Years in US—self	P	16231	1.035	0.237	.926	(.352)
	S	595	1.044	0.270		
Father's occupation	P	13045	8.350	4.149	-.958	(.337)
	S	472	8.167	4.157		
Mother's occupation	P	13657	8.552	5.630	-.425	(.667)
	S	501	8.445	5.445		
Father's education	P	12268	4.660	2.561	.292	(.772)
	S	455	4.695	2.570		
Mother's education	P	13748	4.178	2.170	.371	(.711)
	S	499	4.214	2.210		
Income	P	13861	4.287	1.663	.710	(.478)
	S	516	4.339	1.689		
Own study place	P	14832	1.548	0.498	.937	(.437)
	S	544	1.568	0.496		
Newspaper	P	14916	1.182	0.386	.060	(.952)
	S	545	1.183	0.383		
Encyclopedia	P	14921	1.109	0.312	-1.120	(.263)
	S	527	1.216	0.412		

Table 5 (continued)

Anglo

Item	P/S	N	Mean	Sd	z	(p)
Typewriter	P	14890	1.237	0.425	-.110	(.913)
	S	544	1.235	0.425		
Dishwasher	P	14768	1.383	0.486	-.524	(.603)
	S	537	1.372	0.484		
Two or more cars	P	14905	1.156	0.363	-.321	(.749)
	S	544	1.151	0.358		
50 or more books	P	14864	1.132	0.339	.757	(.447)
	S	544	1.143	0.352		
Own room	P	14912	1.201	0.401	-.524	(.603)
	S	546	1.192	0.394		
Calculator	P	14876	1.163	0.370	-.883	(.379)
	S	545	1.149	0.356		
Father monitor school	P	14792	1.222	0.415	1.183	(.238)
	S	547	1.243	0.429		
Mother monitor school	P	15725	1.114	0.318	1.509	(.131)
	S	576	1.134	0.341		
Plan program w/father	P	15895	1.988	0.687	-.106	(.912)
	S	584	1.985	0.714		
Plan program w/mother	P	16001	2.262	0.636	-.038	(.968)
	S	589	2.261	0.639		
Positive attd self	P	14252	1.865	0.601	-.762	(.447)
	S	525	1.836	0.549		
Person of worth	P	14375	1.808	0.569	.160	(.873)
	S	521	1.812	0.591		
Able to do things	P	14864	1.819	0.562	.877	(.379)
	S	551	1.840	0.594		
Not pay to plan ahead	P	14498	3.001	0.774	.922	(.358)
	S	530	3.032	0.778		
Accept conditions	P	13661	2.446	0.863	-.285	(.772)
	S	499	2.435	0.851		
Good luck not work	P	14456	3.141	0.680	-.577	(.562)
	S	533	3.124	0.671		
Interested in school	P	15625	1.262	0.440	-1.035	(.298)
	S	575	1.243	0.430		
Like work in school	P	15485	1.496	0.500	-1.095	(.271)
	S	567	1.473	0.500		
Vocabulary	P	15292	11.505	4.052	.851	(.395)
	S	566	11.650	4.048		
Reading	P	15271	9.554	3.773	.542	(.589)
	S	566	9.640	3.942		
Writing	P	15000	10.818	3.772	.119	(.904)
	S	558	10.837	3.846		

Table 5 (continued)

Anglo

Item	P/S	N	Mean	Sd	z	(p)
Math–Part I	P	15233	15.125	5.698	2.347	(.019)*
	S	564	15.688	5.820		
Math–Part II	P	15097	4.502	2.072	.903	(.368)
	S	561	4.581	2.173		
Science	P	15124	11.645	3.452	1.113	(.258)
	S	562	11.810	3.469		

Note. All computations are based on original coded values in the HSB data set. Values in parentheses are probabilities associated with the z-values. For each item, "P" refers to population and "S" refers to random sample.
* $p < .05$.

Exploratory Factor Analysis

In order to identify which items on the survey measured which of the three indicators of psychological orientation (i.e., self-concept, internal locus of control, and motivation), exploratory factor analysis (EFA) was performed for each of the three ethnic groups. The purpose was to determine whether the nineteen items which, by the way they were phrased, were designed specifically to measure one of these three psychological factors indeed turned out to measure that designated factor. Only those items which were found to be simple (i.e., loading on one single factor), meaningful (i.e., loading greater than .30), and consistent measures of the respective factors across all three groups were included in the construction of these indicator variables for further LISREL analyses.

For all these exploratory factor analyses, the number of factors was set at three to correspond to the three hypothesized psychological factors. Each factor solution was first rotated using a Varimax orthogonal transformation, followed by a Promax oblique rotation. For comparison purposes, both the unit-erated and iterated procedures were used for factor extraction. Both procedures identified a common set of items for measuring the three factors. Since the iterative procedure tended to produce a "clearner" factor solution, only the results from the iterative procedure are reported here. The resulting three-factor solutions by group are reported in Table 6.

Table 6
EFA Factor Loadings of Potential Items for
Psychological Orientation

	Group								
	Asian (N = 117)			Hispanic (N = 248)			Anglo (N =374)		
	Factor			Factor			Factor		
	I	II	III	I	II	III	I	II	III
Self-Concept									
* 1. CONCPSEF	.609	-.097	.238	.420	.043	.219	.648	-.010	-.030
* 2. CONCPWOR	.731	.109	-.018	.736	-.037	-.075	.658	-.104	.120
* 3. CONCPABL	.702	.145	-.089	.690	.100	-.081	.616	-.062	.117
4. CONCPSAT	.331	-.099	.397	.407	-.265	.305	.463	.188	-.115
5. CONCPGD	.131	.063	.245	.179	.205	.173	.136	.328	-.026
6. CONCPPRD	.306	.380	.135	.353	.301	-.090	.223	.504	.023
Internal Locus of Control									
* 7. CONTRLUK	-.015	.450	.078	.012	.523	-.048	-.054	.354	.219
* 8. CONTRPLN	.050	.516	.185	.035	.494	.112	-.108	.690	.056
* 9. CONTRACC	-.110	.457	-.088	-.044	.517	-.045	-.025	.155	.104
10. CONTRSTP	-.113	.660	.192	.557	-.021	.207	.027	.546	-.026
11. CONTRWK	.513	-.127	.030	.335	-.055	.207	.458	.165	-.060
12. CONTRDO	.440	-.148	-.148	.282	.011	-.119	.295	.065	-.216
Motivation									
*13. MOTSCH	.022	-.135	.597	-.141	-.019	.519	-.030	.032	.631
*14. MOTWORK	-.076	.055	.643	.096	.061	.336	.028	.068	.571
15. MOTED	.092	-.101	.311	.012	.053	.480	.045	.176	.183
16. MOTMATH1	-.011	.182	.358	.132	.218	-.183	-.105	.071	.206
17. MOTMATH2	.046	.519	-.129	-.031	-.036	.179	-.017	.043	.327
18. MOTENGL1	-.125	.037	.500	-.015	.131	-.037	.039	-.028	.174
19. MOTENGL2	.001	.463	-.260	.083	.103	-.010	-.131	.090	.112
Eigenvalue	3.027	1.878	0.998	2.104	1.366	.740	2.354	1.288	.851

Note. All factor solutions are obtained from a Promax oblique rotation using iterated factor extraction procedure. Items marked with a leading asterisk are retained for constructing their repective latent constructs.

The items in Table 6 are arranged in clusters of the three theoretical factors. Those that turned out to measure their hypothesized factors consistently across groups are marked with a leading asterisk. It can be clearly seen that of the six items presumably measuring self-concept, only the first three—"Positive attitude toward self (CONCPSEF)," "Person of worth (CONCPWOR)," "Able to do things as well as others (CONCPABL)"—were consistent measures of self-concept. Item 4 "Satisfied with self (CONCPSAT)" was not a consistent measure of self-concept across groups. Item 5 "No good at all (CONCPGD)" was not a meaningful measure of any of the three factors (i.e., loadings were small). Item 6 "Nothing to be proud (CONCPPRD)" tended to load on multiple factors (I and II). Therefore, the decision was to retain CONCPSEF, CONCPWOR, and CONCPABL in forming the composite CONCPT.

Of the six items presumably measuring internal locus of control, the first three items—"Luck more important (CONTRLUK)," "Plans hardly work (CONTRPLN)," and "Should accept conditions (CONTACC)"—turned out to be simple, meaningful, and consistent measures across groups, although the third item only loaded very weakly (.155) on this factor for the Anglo group. Item 10 "Someone stops me (CONTRSTP)" failed the consistency requirement. The last two items—"My plans work (CONTRWK)," and "What happens is my own doing (CONTRDO)"—turned out to be, rather unexpectedly, measures of self-concept. Rather than including them in the construction of self-concept, they were dropped from this study for lack of theoretical ground.

The seven items which were presumed to measure academic motivation exhibited very confusing and inconsistent patterns of factor loadings. Only the first two items—"Satisfied with school (MOTSCH)" and "Enjoy working hard (MOTWORK)"—were good measures of motivation. Item 15 "Satisfied with education (MOTED)" did not produce meaningful loadings for the Anglo group. No generalization can be made about the other four items relating to attitudes toward Math and English (MOTMATH1, MOTMATH2, MOTENGL1, MOTENGL2). They were simply dropped from further analysis. As such, the first two items were really measures of attitude rather than motivation. It should therefore be borne in mind that the word "motivation" in this study takes on a slightly different meaning from its conventional definition.

The resulting eight items were then once again factor analyzed to determine their factor structures, the eigenvalues associated with these factors, the communalities and corresponding errors of unreliabilities of the eight items. The results are summarized in Tables 7 and 8.

As expected, the factor loadings in Table 7 fairly closely satisfied Thurstone's (1947, p. 335) criteria for "simple structure." Again, the factor solutions obtained from the uniterated and iterated procedures were very similar to each other. The first three items unambiguously loaded on self-concept, the second three items on locus on control, and the last two on motivation. It should be noted, however, that the item "Accept conditions" did not turn out to be a good measure of any of the three factors for the Anglo as none of its loadings reached .3—the conventionally adopted minimal loading considered meaningful.

In all cases, factor I can be labelled as self-concept. In most cases, factor II can be labelled as motivation and factor III as internal locus of control, except for the Hispanic group's uniterated solutions, which produced factor II as internal locus of control and factor III as motivation.

Turning to the eigenvalues, or the variances explained by the factors, we can see that in all cases, self-concept was the most reliable indicator of psychological orientation, as its eigenvalue uniformly turned out to be the largest. Internal locus of control, on the other hand, was a poorer measure of psychological orientation. However, in no case did the variance explained by internal locus of control come less than half of that of self-concept.

The reliabilities (or communalities) and their corresponding unreliabilities[6] (or errors of measurement) of the individual items are reported in Table 8. Not surprisingly, the reliabilities were generally not very impressive. In fact, most of the reliability indices were smaller than the unreliability indices. The items measuring internal locus of control had the lowest reliabilities, particularly with "Luck important" (between .178 and .265) and "Accept conditions" (between .025 and .338). The item behaving most satisfactorily and consistently was "Person

Table 7
EFA Factor Loadings of Identified Items for Psychological Orientation

	Asian (N = 117)			Hispanic (N = 248)			Anglo (N = 374)		
	Factor			Factor			Factor		
	I	II	III	I	II	III	I	II	III
SELF-CONCEPT									
Positive twd. self	.591	.199	-.085	.437	.008	.061	.515	-.013	-.001
Person of worth	.864	-.092	-.020	.675	-.057	-.074	.738	.028	.018
Able to do things	.641	-.049	.057	.738	.029	.058	.728	.008	.027
INTERNAL LOCUS OF CONTROL									
Luck important	-.013	.006	.487	.044	-.032	.435	.047	.165	.372
Not pay to plan	.073	.154	.706	.083	-.040	.469	-.031	-.002	.883
Accept conditions	-.093	-.164	.378	-.078	.056	.611	.047	-.036	.144
MOTIVATION									
Satisfied w/ sch.	-.015	.813	-.104	.056	.811	-.027	-.030	.960	-.025
Like working hard	-.009	.535	.099	-.065	.453	.010	.047	.407	.074
Eigenvalue	1.636	1.232	.992	1.280	.977	.805	1.389	1.163	.997

Note. All factor solutions are obtained from a Promax oblique rotation using iterated factor extraction procedure.

of worth" measuring self-concept, with reliabilities ranging from .375 to .704.

In sum, the exploratory factor analyses successfully identified eight items as simple, meaningful, and consistent measures of self-concept, internal locus of control, and motivation. Although most of their reliabilities fell short of what would be conventionally accepted as appropriate (.70 or greater), they were judged as reasonably satisfactory, considering they were reliabilities of *single* items.

Simple Statistics of Indicator Variables

The simple statistics of the eighteen indicator variables are summarized in Table 9. In addition to N's, means, and stan-

Table 8
Communalities and Unreliabilities of Identified Items for Psychological Orientation

	Group					
	Asian		Hispanic		Anglo	
	Comm.	Unrel.	Comm.	Unrel.	Comm.	Unrel.
SELF-CONCEPT						
Positive twd. self	.443	.557	.196	.804	.263	.737
Person of worth	.704	.296	.444	.556	.554	.446
Able to do things	.408	.592	.561	.439	.533	.467
INTERNAL LOCUS OF CONTROL						
Luck important	.236	.764	.188	.812	.185	.815
Not pay to plan	.598	.402	.222	.778	.774	.226
Accept conditions	.149	.851	.388	.612	.025	.975
MOTIVATION						
Satisfied w/ sch.	.627	.373	.194	.806	.913	.087
Like working hard	.317	.683	.682	.318	.184	.816
Total community	3.483		2.875		3.430	

dard deviations, this table also reports skewness, kurtosis, and D-statistic for testing univariate normality. The mean describes the central tendency of a distribution; the standard deviation, the variability. The skewness measures the degree of asymmetry; the kurtosis, the degree of peakness. The D-statistic and its associated p-value tests the null hypothesis that the data are from a normal distribution. It is appropriate when the sample size is greater than 50 (Stephens, 1974).

Because the means usually provide the key information about the data, we shall now turn to them for a closer examination. In the discussion that follows, the means are interpreted in light of the recoded scales of the composite variables. (Please refer to the section on Variables in Chapter Two for more information). Whenever appropriate, comparisons are made on the three group means. Bearing in mind that no significance test

Results

Table 9
Simple Statistics of Indicator Variables

Variable	Mini-mum	Maxi-mum	Group	Mean	Sd	Skew	Kurt.	D	p <
Ethnic Language Dominance									
1. ELCHILD	1	3	Asian	2.17	0.80	-0.32	-0.47	0.08	.01
			Hisp	2.08	0.63	-0.06	-0.46	0.31	.01
			Anglo	—	—	—	—	—	—
2. CURREL	10	50	Asian	22.61	10.21	1.53	-0.75	0.15	.01
			Hisp	27.62	9.54	0.14	-0.85	0.08	.01
			Anglo	—	—	—	—	—	—
3. YRSUS	-14	-3	Asian	-9.36	3.99	0.07	-1.36	0.14	.01
			Hisp	-13.23	2.76	1.69	2.18	0.31	.01
			Anglo	—	—	—	—	—	—
4. ELABL	4	16	Asian	9.85	3.94	0.28	-1.15	0.12	.01
			Hisp	11.58	3.01	-0.36	-0.41	0.12	.01
			Anglo	—	—	—	—	—	—
Socio-Economic Status									
5. PAROCC	21.5	72.8	Asian	84.61	20.40	-0.51	-0.12	0.08	.07
			Hisp	66.49	24.12	0.12	-0.55	0.11	.01
			Anglo	76.97	25.52	-0.06	-0.46	0.07	.01
6. PARED	11	19	Asian	25.64	6.31	-0.43	-0.03	0.12	.01
			Hisp	20.75	5.96	-0.41	-0.38	0.31	.01
			Anglo	23.69	6.49	-0.30	-0.17	0.18	.01
7. HOUSPOSS	0	9	Asian	7.05	1.59	-0.76	0.42	0.17	.01
			Hisp	5.35	2.07	-0.12	-0.82	0.11	.01
			Anglo	6.91	1.60	-0.92	1.19	0.17	.01
8. INCOME	3.5	45	Asian	21.86	11.86	0.98	0.07	0.23	.01
			Hisp	15.59	8.65	1.21	2.21	0.18	.01
			Anglo	22.37	10.91	0.73	-0.15	0.21	.01
Parental Involvement									
9. PARSCHL	2	4	Asian	1.68	0.67	-1.87	1.93	0.48	.01
			Hisp	1.60	0.64	-1.38	0.69	0.42	.01
			Anglo	1.59	0.69	-1.39	0.47	0.43	.01
10. PARPLAN	2	6	Asian	4.47	1.19	-0.24	-0.69	0.22	.01
			Hisp	4.17	1.22	-0.12	-0.64	0.20	.01
			Anglo	4.33	1.14	-0.18	-0.54	0.21	.01

Table 9 (continued)

Variable	Mini-mum	Maxi-mum	Group	Mean	Sd	Skew	Kurt.	D	p <
Psychological Orientation									
11. CONCPT	3	12	Asian	9.51	2.08	-1.17	1.74	0.23	.01
			Hisp	8.83	2.23	-0.79	0.31	0.23	.01
			Anglo	9.10	1.96	-1.00	1.52	0.24	.01
12. CONTRL	3	12	Asian	8.10	2.18	-0.80	0.53	0.18	.01
			Hisp	7.37	2.20	-0.58	0.20	0.16	.01
			Anglo	8.19	1.97	-0.69	0.50	0.18	.01
13. MOT	0	2	Asian	1.62	0.64	-1.44	0.87	0.43	.01
			Hisp	1.45	0.73	-0.93	-0.52	0.37	.01
			Anglo	1.35	0.74	-0.66	-0.90	0.32	.01
Verbal Achievement									
14. VOCAB	0	21	Asian	11.74	4.94	-0.16	-0.92	0.11	.01
			Hisp	9.16	4.09	0.42	-0.32	0.11	.01
			Anglo	12.33	4.00	-0.30	-0.41	0.08	.01
15. READING	0	21	Asian	10.07	4.29	-0.08	-0.92	0.08	.08
			Hisp	7.81	3.46	0.70	0.29	0.11	.01
			Anglo	10.42	3.96	0.14	-0.67	0.09	.01
16. WRITING	0	17	Asian	12.25	3.65	-0.70	-0.47	0.16	.01
			Hisp	9.12	3.36	0.07	-0.62	0.09	.01
			Anglo	11.47	3.67	-0.46	-0.54	0.11	.01
Quantitative Achievement									
17. MATH	0	38	Asian	23.85	7.72	-0.23	-0.72	0.07	.15
			Hisp	15.49	6.43	0.86	0.45	0.14	.01
			Anglo	21.38	7.29	-0.02	-0.79	0.06	.01
18. SCIENCE	0	20	Asian	11.94	3.58	-0.40	-0.61	0.13	.01
			Hisp	9.19	3.45	-0.18	-0.45	0.08	.01
			Anglo	12.30	3.39	-0.20	-0.47	0.08	.01

Note. N for Asian = 117; N for Hispanic = 248; N for Anglo = 374. Minimum and maximum refer to possible values, not actual response values.

was performed on those mean comparisons, the findings should be interpreted as purely descriptive and not inferential.

Variable 1 ELCHILD measures the degree of monolingualism during childhood, and was coded as 1 representing mono-

English, 2 representing bilingual, and 3 representing mono-ethnic language. Therefore the larger the mean, the more frequent use of the ethnic language. It appears that both the Asian and Hispanic students made equal use of their ethnic language and English, although the Asian students (2.17) tended to rely a little more on their ethnic language than the Hispanic (2.08).

Variable 2 CURREL measures the frequency of ethnic language use at the time of the survey. The results show that both groups used their ethnic language only occasionally (22.61 for the Asian and 27.62 for the Hispanic). An interesting contrast is that while the Hispanic tended to make more frequent use of English during their childhood than the Asian, this tendency reversed during later years, as is suggested by the higher mean of CURREL for the Hispanic compared to that for the Asian.

Variable 3 YRSUS measures the length of residency in the U.S. The scores were converted to their negatives to reflect the length of residency as a negative function of ethnic-language dominance. Here we see quite a difference between the Asian and the Hispanic. While the Asian (-9.36) indicated that they or their parents had spent more than 10 years but less than all of their lives in the U.S., the Hispanic (-13.23) indicated having spent all or almost all of their lives here.

Variable 4 ELABL measures the self-reported proficiency level of the ethnic language. Both groups indicated a fair command of their ethnic language, but the Hispanic (11.58), perhaps because of their more frequent use, tended to claim greater proficiency in their ethnic language than the Asian (9.85).

Turning to social-economic status, we see the Asian group leading the other two on parental occupation (84.61), parental education (25.64), and household possessions (7.05). When it comes to monetary reward, however, the Asian (21.86) were not as well off as the Anglo (22.37). On all SES measures, the Hispanic scored the lowest.

In terms of parental involvement in academic study, the Asian parents had the highest degree of school monitoring (1.68), and the Anglo the lowest (1.59), although the differences between groups were relatively small. On a similar measure of parental monitoring in planning high school program, again the Asian parents were most involved (4.47), and the Hispanic least (4.17).

On variables measuring psychological orientation, all three groups responded quite positively. The Asian group indicated most positive orientation toward themselves (9.51) and school (1.62), but they did not feel as much in control of their environments as the Anglo (8.10 for Asian and 8.19 for Anglo). Although the Anglo had a slight edge over the Hispanic on self-concept (9.10 for Anglo and 8.83 for Hispanic) and internal locus of control (8.19 for Anglo and 7.37 for Hispanic), they tended to be less academically motivated (1.35 for Anglo and 1.45 for Hispanic).

On measures of verbal achievement, the Anglo had a slight edge over the Asian on vocabulary (12.33 over 11.74) and reading (10.42 over 10.07), but the situation is reversed on writing (12.25 for Asian and 11.47 for Anglo). On all three measures the Hispanic scored the lowest, and the discrepancies were fairly sizeable.

On measures of quantitative achievement, the Asian outperformed the Anglo on mathematics (23.85 over 21.38); whereas the Anglo surpassed the Asian on science (12.30 over 11.94). Again, the lowest-scoring group was Hispanic.

Turning now to the D-statistics for test of univariate normality, we see a somewhat alerting situation—all but three (PAROCC, READING, MATH) of the eighteen test statistics turned out to be significant at alpha = .01. Rejection to the null hypothesis leads to the conclusion that the majority of the eighteen indicator variables were drawn from non-normal distributions. The problem, then, would be to determine how serious the departure from multivariate normal distribution was and whether transformation was necessary to approximate multivariate normality.

As has been discussed in Chapter Two, when the sample size and the number of variables are large, it is neither feasible nor desirable to conduct a multivariate normality test. Univariate distributions should fairly accurately represent their joint multivariate distribution. Bearing this in mind, then, should the results of the univariate normally reported in Table 9 be taken as serious violation of this assumption?

I suggest "no" for two reasons. One, most of those D-statistics were significant at $p < .01$. It is a well known statistical artifact that when the sample size is small, only the most aberrant behavior will be identified as lack of fit, whereas very large samples almost invariantly produce statistically significant lack of fit, even though the departure from the specified distribution may be very small and technically unimportant to the inferential conclusions (Johnson & Wichern, 1982). Therefore, those significant D-values do not necessarily indicate large departure from normal distribution. Two, none of the skewness statistics were greater than 2 in absolute value. It has been empirically shown that LISREL estimation has a high tolerance level for skewness within the range of -2 to +2 when the numbers of categories of the ordinal variables are greater than four (Muthen, 1982). Based on the above two observations, the decision was made to proceed with subsequent multivariate analyses without transformation.

Correlations and Generalized Variances
The zero-order correlation matrix of the eighteen indicator variables for each group is presented in Table 10. The matrix can be viewed as consisting of several blocks of cells according to the six latent constructs they were hypothesized to measure.

Starting with ethnic-language dominance, we can see that all four variables were moderately to highly correlated (ranging from .228 to .742), lending strong support to the observation that the more frequent use of ethnic language during childhood and the shorter the period of residency in the U.S., the more likely that the child will continue to rely on the ethnic language into adulthood, and to develop proficiency in that ethnic language. This tendency seems to be stronger for the Asian (ranging from .459 to .742) than the Hispanic (ranging from .228 to .527).

Looking down the blocks related to ethnic-language dominance (columns 1, 2, 3, and 4), we see a consistent negative association between ethnic-language dominance and all the

Table 10
Correlations Among Indicator Variables

	1	2	3	4	5	6	7
1. ELCHILD	—						
2. CURREL	.539 / .501	—					
3. YRSUS	.647 / .434	.596 / .228	—				
4. ELABL	.459 / .459	.742 / .527	.547 / .322	—			
5. PAROCC	-.148 / -.113	-.040 / -.116	-.066 / -.181	-.176 / -.092	—		
6. PARED	.051 / -.138	.142 / -.122	.119 / -.175	.121 / -.126	.265 / .335 / .514	—	
7. POSSESS	-.196 / -.242	-.104 / -.271	-.258 / -.259	-.132 / -.130	-.132 / .316 / .291	.316 / .247 / .304	—

Table 10 (continued)

	1	2	3	4	5	6	7	8	9	10	11	12	13	14	15
8. INCOME	-.176	-.210	-.125	-.106	.311	.301	.310	—							
	-.123	-.225	.083	-.183	.249	.211	.387								
	—	—	—	—	.303	.294	.405								
9. PARSCHL	-.011	.070	.116	.038	.113	.043	.056	.011	—						
	-.118	.032	-.165	-.107	.259	.222	.223	.114							
	—	—	—	—	.181	.117	.080	.028							
10. PARPLAN	-.175	.078	-.091	.110	.220	.243	.295	.088	.406	—					
	-.066	-.030	-.002	-.031	.179	.164	.178	.109	.401						
	—	—	—	—	.220	.272	.310	.191	.304						
11. CONCPT	-.048	.083	-.008	.042	-.034	.077	.224	.010	.143	.090	—				
	-.036	-.066	.038	.100	.022	.158	.169	.135	.122	.283					
	—	—	—	—	.122	.099	.125	.122	.078	.108					
12. CONTRL	-.050	-.245	-.149	-.231	.011	.202	.192	.207	.017	.117	.132	—			
	.042	-.064	.082	.123	-.001	-.016	.046	.054	-.025	.009	.163				
	—	—	—	—	.144	.067	.063	.119	.045	.229	.196				
13. MOT	.112	.152	.050	.063	.006	.187	.112	.039	.359	.261	.330	.102	—		
	.022	-.018	.063	.111	.029	.014	.084	.067	.089	.216	.108	.120			
	—	—	—	—	.079	.063	.161	.091	.194	.236	.059	.145			
14. VOCAB	-.287	-.382	-.339	-.441	.220	.130	.329	.289	-.093	.203	.178	.455	.064	—	
	-.113	-.321	-.011	-.047	.133	.137	.085	.147	.016	.043	.119	.262	.083		
	—	—	—	—	.342	.232	.302	.187	.022	.187	.163	.357	.123		
15. READ	-.196	-.281	-.372	-.380	.117	.125	.342	.336	-.014	.115	.183	.449	.110	.812	—
	-.037	-.219	-.029	-.115	.116	.142	.115	.108	-.023	.111	.070	.275	.084	.617	
	—	—	—	—	.335	.254	.288	.147	.015	.170	.143	.381	.149	.731	

Table 10 (continued)

The first value in each cell refers to the Asian group; the second to the Hispanic; the third to the Anglo group. Values are stacked in each cell.

	1	2	3	4	5	6	7	8	9	10	11	12	13	14	15	16	17	18
16. WRITE	-.156 / .062 / —	-.164 / -.304 / —	-.254 / .082 / —	-.265 / -.124 / —	.146 / .201 / .301	.203 / .126 / .136	.250 / .174 / .250	.262 / .152 / .077	-.003 / .050 / .012	.070 / .126 / .130	.306 / .066 / .135	.444 / .213 / .373	.207 / .113 / .151	.601 / .554 / .592	.717 / .535 / .619	—		
17. MATH	-.029 / .057 / —	-.080 / -.178 / —	-.070 / .022 / —	-.023 / -.047 / —	.117 / .158 / .332	.177 / .133 / .270	.254 / .165 / .222	.276 / .222 / .137	-.043 / .017 / .010	.058 / .138 / .195	.183 / .101 / .163	.339 / .254 / .382	.125 / .115 / .222	.479 / .499 / .623	.607 / .569 / .677	.551 / .611 / .595	—	
18. SCIENCE	-.122 / .037 / —	-.148 / -.162 / —	-.253 / -.024 / —	-.257 / -.076 / —	.183 / .172 / .289	.148 / .137 / .231	.235 / .110 / .164	.225 / .184 / .141	-.143 / .052 / -.033	.136 / .135 / .121	.275 / .067 / .184	.435 / .228 / .340	.129 / .043 / .098	.673 / .578 / .634	.730 / .639 / .656	.653 / .581 / .561	.791 / .589 / .659	—

Note. The first value in each cell refers to the Asian group (N = 117); the second to the Hispanic (N = 248); the third to the Anglo (N = 374). For the Asian group, all correlations greater than .183 are significant at alpha = .05 and values greater than .243 are significant at .01. For the Hispanic group, all correlations greater than .126 are significant at alpha = .05 and values greater than .164 are significant at .01. For the Anglo group, correlations greater than .110 are significant at alpha = .05 and values greater than .135 are significant at .01.

other latent constructs, but the strength was relatively weak, with the correlations ranging from .040 to .269 in absolute value. That ethnic-language dominance was negatively correlated with socio-economic status is hardly surprising as has been frequently reported in studies on language minority issues. What is not clear from these data is whether indeed the use of ethnic language "caused" low SES, or whether it was something else, such as ethnicity. This question will be addressed more fully in the covariance structure analyses later in this chapter.

Relationship between ethnic-language dominance and parental involvement is less clearcut. Most of the correlations were very low (.002 to .175 in magnitude), and the directions were inconsistent. The same can be said about the relationship between ethnic language dominance and psychological orientation. The magnitudes of the correlations were between .008 to .245, and about half of them were positive and the other half negative.

Perhaps the most disturbing finding in these data is the relationship between ethnic-language dominance and academic achievement. Although not strong in magnitude, the correlations were overwhelmingly negative for the Asian (from -.023 to -.441), and also for the Hispanic, with only one or two minor exceptions (from -.304 to .022). The association was stronger for verbal achievement (with a mean correlation of -.210) than quantitative achievement (mean correlation = -.132).

We now turn to the second set of blocks (columns 5, 6, 7, and 8), starting with the correlations among the four measures of SES. Parental education and occupation appear to be only slightly to moderately correlated with household possession and family income (.132 to .514). The mismatch between education and earning was most conspicuous for the Hispanic (.211), and so was that between occupation and earning (.249). The finding suggests that racial discrimination against the Hispanic may still be very much a reality in today's job market. Again, such observation can not be confirmed without further scrutinization of related variables such as personality traits, cultural beliefs, etc.

Correlations between SES and parental involvement were all small and positive, ranging from .043 to .310. This runs parallel to the assumption that parents who are socio-economically better off tend to be more concerned about their children's academic life than those who must struggle for a living. But the evidence is not substantial.

Much the same can be said about the relationship between SES and psychological orientation. The correlations ranged from -.034 to .224, with the majority being small and positive.

Relationship between SES and academic achievement was not a strong one either. The correlations were between .077 to .342, but most of them were statistically significant.

The third set of blocks (columns 9 and 10) deals with the relationship between parental involvement, psychological orientation, and academic achievement. The degree of parental concern did not seem to relate substantially to self-concept (.078 to .203) or internal locus of control (-.025 to .229), but did seem to play a more important role in motivation (.089 to .359).

Finally, the relationship between parental involvement and academic achievement was in most cases small and insignificant. The correlations were between -.149 and .195, with the majority closer to zero.

Turning now to the fourth set of blocks (columns 11, 12, and 13), we see only small correlations among the three measures of psychological orientation (.059 to .330). This suggests that the three variables (self-concept, internal locus of control, and motivation) may be poor measures of the same underlying construct (psychological orientation). Stronger argument for this observation is provided by the confirmatory factor analysis in the following section.

On the relationship between psychological orientation and academic achievement, we see a fairly strong bond (.043 and .485), with a mean of .210 for the verbal and .207 for the quantitative. Of the three measures of psychological orientation, internal locus of control was most highly correlated with achievement (ranging from .213 to .485), particularly so for the Asian.

Lastly, we turn to the relationship between verbal and quantitative achievements (columns 14 through 18). Verbal and quantitative achievements appear to be quite highly correlated (ranging from .479 to .730). Somewhat surprising was that this association held equally strong for Anglo group (.561 to .677), as we would expect the quantitative performance of Anglo students to be influenced by their verbal ability by a lesser degree than language minority students. Based on this preliminary finding, then, the assumption that no relationship existed between verbal and quantitative achievements for the Anglo group would have to be challenged. Therefore the decision was made to test the plausibility of adding a causal path from verbal to quantitative achievement for the Anglo group.

In sum, based on the zero-order correlations among the eighteen indicator variables, we would expect ethnic language and psychological orientation to play a stronger role than SES or parental involvement in determining academic achievement.

Before proceeding with the covariance structure analysis, it is usually a good practice to examine the generalized variance of the correlations of interest. Computed as the determinant of a correlation matrix, the generalized variance indicates the orthogonality, or conversely, multicollinearity of the correlation matrix. It provides preliminary information about the "ill-conditioning" of the matrix (Jöreskog & Sörbom, 1984, p. III.8) and whether LISREL's maximum likelihood estimation would be possible. A value close to zero indicates low orthogonality or high multicollinearity, and ML estimation would not be applicable. As a rule of thumb, the index should not be smaller than 1×10^{-6} or 1×10^{-7} (Bachman, personal communication, June 1987).

The generalized variances of the various sets of correlation coefficients used in this study are reported in Table 11. It is clear that none of them was small enough to raise a concern. In fact, the preceding discussion on the correlations among the eighteen indicator variables already lent partial support to this finding, as the majority of the inter-correlations were not very strong. The ML estimation should therefore be well justified in this regard.

Confirmatory Factor Analysis

As a precursory step to covariance structure modeling, confirmatory factor analysis (CFA) was performed to examine the fac-

Table 11
Generalized Variances of Correlations

	Group		
	Asian (N = 117)	Hispanic (N = 248)	Anglo (N = 374)
Exogenous	.07788	.21320	.51224
Endogenous	.01034	.06102	.03207
Total	.00021	.00683	.00887

tor structures and reliabilities and validities of the measurement models for the exogenous variables and endogenous variables separately. A common CFA model was sought that would fit all three groups optimally so that multi-group modeling would be possible.

Specification Search
As it turned out, the process of searching for a common, optimal-fitting CFA model for the three groups was not easy—such a model simply did not exist. For example, relaxing a fixed parameter might significantly improve the fit for one group but decrease the fit for another. Therefore efforts were made to strive for a common model that fit all three groups reasonably well, although that model might not be the best-fitting one for any one group among a few known alternates.

Table 12 summarizes the searching process described above. For both the exogenous and endogenous variables, the initial models assumed a simple factor structure; i.e., the indicators loaded on their respective underlying factors only, and no complex-loading was allowed. Turning first to the exogenous variables, the results were less than satisfactory—the lack of fit was significant at alpha = .01 for both the Asian and the Hispanic, although the goodness-of-fit index (GFI) and adjusted GFI were both close or above .90. The root mean-square residual (RMSR) was somewhat higher for the Asian (.092) than for the Hispanic

Table 12
Specification Search in CFA Modeling

Model	χ^2	df	p	GFI	Adj. GFI	RMSR	χ^2/df
			Exogenous Variables				
Asian (N = 117)							
1. Simple	51.50	19	.000	.903	.817	.092	2.689
2. Modified	37.94	18	.004	.925	.850	.052	2.108
Hispanic (N = 248)							
1. Simple	43.80	19	.001	.958	.921	.051	2.305
2. Modified	43.79	18	.001	.958	.917	.051	2.433
			Endogenous Variables				
Asian (N = 117)							
1. Simple	63.72	29	.000	.899	.809	.092	2.197
2. Modified	52.31	28	.004	.918	.838	.073	1.868
Hispanic (N = 248)							
1. Simple	43.68	29	.039	.967	.937	.048	1.506
2. Modified	25.70	28	.590	.980	.961	.025	0.918
Anglo (N = 374)							
1. Simple	40.81	29	.071	.978	.959	.038	1.407
2. Modified	35.92	28	.145	.981	.963	.036	1.283

(.051). The χ^2/df ratio was only marginally acceptable (2.689 for the Asian and 2.305 for the Hispanic). Therefore the decision was to look for a better-fitting model.

In the process of specification search, the modification indices provide the primary source of empirical guidance. Reported in Table 13 are the five largest modification indices at each step of the searching process. The largest modification indices occurred in the TD (Theta Delta) matrix. Although relaxing TD(4,2), which is the correlation between the measurement errors of ELABL and CURREL, appeared to be the most effective way of improving the fit (20.811 for the Asian and 19.326 for the Hispanic), it was not recommended for lack of theoretical support. The decision was to relax LX(6,1)

Table 13
Modification Indices of CFA Modeling

			Group				
	Asian		Hispanic			Anglo	

Exogenous Variables

Model 1 (simple)

	Label	MI		Label	MI		
1.	TD(4,2)	20.811		TD(3,2)	15.484		
2.	TD(3,1)	19.667		TD(4,2)	10.766		
3.	LX(6,1)	11.863		TD(3,1)	9.242		
4.	TD(4,1)	6.528		TD(6,5)	8.026		
5.	TD(8,3)	6.776		LX(3,2)	4.215		

Model 2 (modified)

	Label	MI		Label	MI		
1.	TD(4,2)	19.326		TD(3,2)	15.484		
2.	TD(3,1)	18.850		TD(4,2)	10.766		
3.	TD(5,1)	6.868		TD(3,1)	9.242		
4.	TD(8,3)	6.233		TD(6,5)	8.026		
5.	TD(4,3)	3.488		LX(3,2)	4.215		

Endogenous Variables

Model 1 (simple)

	Label	MI	Label	MI		Label	MI
1.	LX(5,4)	9.855	LX(4,1)	16.174		LX(5,1)	7.862
2.	LX(3,3)	9.688	LX(4,3)	13.199		TD(5,1)	7.836
3.	LX(5,1)	9.589	LX(4,4)	11.747		TD(9,5)	6.425
4.	LX(4,1)	8.189	TD(4,2)	11.130		LX(4,3)	4.457
5.	TD(5,3)	8.093	TD(9,8)	8.358		LX(9,2)	4.232

Model 2 (modified)

	Label	MI	Label	MI		Label	MI
1.	TD(6,2)	6.985	TD(9,8)	8.610		TD(5,1)	6.667
2.	TD(10,1)	6.525	TD(8,7)	6.536		TD(9,5)	6.647
3.	LX(1,4)	6.241	TD(9,6)	5.513		LX(1,2)	6.547
4.	TD(7,6)	6.209	TD(7,6)	4.587		LX(2,2)	6.546
5.	TD(5,3)	6.135	TD(6,2)	2.492		LX(1,4)	5.019

instead, which is the factor loading of PARED on ethnic-language dominance. By adding the path from ethnic-language dominance to PARED, it was assumed that parental education was also an indicator of ethnic-language dominance.

Returning to Table 12, we see that this practice, although significantly improved the fit for the Asian (the p-value increased
from .000 to .004), predictably did not bring the desirable effect
to the Hispanic. This already provides some preliminary evidence for rejecting the invariance hypothesis of the factor structures between the two groups. At any rate, the fit for both
groups appears to be acceptable.

Again referring to Table 13 for help on model modification,
we see no clues for improving the model-data fit other than
allowing the measurement errors to correlate. For lack of theoretical justification for relaxing any of these fixed parameters,
the decision was to stop the specification search at this point.
The final CFA model of the exogenous variables fit the Asian
group somewhat better than the Hispanic.

Turning now to the CFA models for the endogenous variables in Table 12, the simple model provided quite a good fit
for the Hispanic (p = .039, χ^2/df = 1.506) and the Anglo (p =
.071, χ^2/df = 1.407), but not quite so for the Asian (p = .000,
χ^2/df = 2.197). Therefore a better-fitting model was sought
after. For information on the modification indices, we again
turn to Table 13.

Because the fit of the Hispanic and Anglo groups was already
very good, the focus was on the Asian group in bringing the fit
to an acceptable level. Of the five top candidates listed for the
Asian group, the fourth one LX(4,1), or the loading of internal
locus of control on parental involvement, was chosen for two
reasons: one, it is theoretically justifiable to claim that locus of
control is also a measure of parental involvement since it is
likely that the more the parents monitor their children's work,
the less the children would feel in control of the environment;
second, relaxing LX(4,1) would also improve the fit significantly
for the Hispanic.

The results of freeing LX(4,1) are quite impressive. The fit
for the Asian improved significantly (the p increased from .000
to .004 and the χ^2/df ratio decreased from 2.197 to 1.868). The
most dramatic improvement was for the Hispanic group, with
the p increasing from .039 to .590, and the χ^2/df ratio
decreasing from 1.506 to 0.918. Even for the Anglo the results
are very encouraging. The p increased from .071 to .145, the

GFI and adjusted GFI were all close to or above .90, the RMSR was controlled under .080, and the χ^2/df ratio decreased from 1.407 to 1.283).

To further explore the possibility of fit improvement, we again consult Table 13 for modification indices. Now we do not see any ideal candidate for further improving the model; so the decision was to stop at this point.

Reliabilities of Indicator Variables

The reliability of an indicator variable, defined as the "squared multiple correlation" (SMC) in LISREL terms, is a measure of the amount of the variance of the underlying factor shared or explained by the indicator variable. It is computed as

$$SMC = 1 - var(e)/var(Y),$$

where var(e) is the variance of the measurement error and var(Y) is the variance of the indicator variable Y. When standardized data are used (i.e., the correlation matrix), var(Y) = 1.0. Therefore the above equation reduces to

$$SMC = 1 - var(e).$$

As such, the reliability is simply the portion of the Y variance that is *not* attributable to measurement error. The reliabilities of both the simple model and the modified model are reported in Table 14.

For the exogenous variables, the reliabilities of the simple model ranged from .196 to .757 for the Asian, from .198 to .525 for the Hispanic, and from .242 to .475 for the Anglo. Modifying the model, although it improved the fit, did not seem to improve the reliabilities (except, of course, PARED for the Asian group, as a result of relaxing the LX(6,1) parameter). In fact, the mean reliability remained exactly the same (.435 for the Asian and .361 for the Hispanic).

As was expected from the discussion on the zero-order correlations, YRSUS turned out to be a relatively poor measure of ethnic-language dominance for the Hispanic (.237). PAROCC had the lowest reliability for the Asian (.181), and PARED for the Hispanic (.196).

Table 14
Reliabilities of Indicator Variables in CFA Models

	Group					
	Asian		Hispanic		Anglo	
	Exogenous Variables					
	Model		Model		Model	
	1	2	1	2	1	2
1. ELCHILD	.428	.433	.525	.525	·	·
2. CURREL	.757	.747	.492	.491	·	·
3. YRSUS	.521	.528	.237	.237	·	·
4. ELABL	.656	.656	.452	.452	·	·
5. PAROCC	.196	.181	.258	.257	.472	·
6. PARED	.234	.463	.198	.196	.475	·
7. INCOME	.447	.356	.284	.285	.243	·
8. HOUSPOSS	.239	.261	.440	.441	.242	·
	Endogenous Variables					
	Model		Model		Model	
	1	2	1	2	1	2
1. PARSCHL	1.877	.699	1.080	.193	.108	.148
2. PARPLAN	.088	.222	.920	.835	.858	.628
3. CONCPT	.124	.121	.110	.094	.074	.065
4. CONTRL	.279	.298	.197	.555	.334	.362
5. MOT	.092	.232	.099	.084	.088	.112
6. VOCAB	.720	.721	.547	.545	.684	.684
7. READ	.891	.889	.614	.617	.755	.755
8. WRITE	.581	.582	.547	.545	.531	.531
9. MATH	.537	.547	.551	.551	.680	.679
10. SCIENCE	.916	.900	.630	.630	.639	.640

For the endogenous variables, some of the reliabilities of the simple model were clearly inadmissible—having a squared multiple correlation of greater than one (1.877 for the Asian and 1.080 for the Hispanic). The only sensible explanation for this phenomenon is that during the maximum likelihood estimation process a relative minimum for the ML function was found, resulting in a negative TD value, thus a corresponding greater-than-one SMC value. This is called a "Heywood case" (Johnson & Wichern, P. 450). Fortunately, this Heywood case phenomenon was eliminated when the model was modified. The resulting reliabilities ranged from .121 to .900 for the Asian group, .084 to .835 for the Hispanic, and .065 to .755 for the Anglo. The mean reliabilities of the endogenous variables were in general higher than those of the exogenous variables, with again the Asian group (mean = .521) higher than the Hispanic (mean = .465) and Anglo (mean = .460).

Reliabilities and Validities of CFA Models
The reliability of a CFA measurement model is defined as the "total coefficient of determination" for all the indicator variables combined. It measures how well the observed variables serve jointly as the measurement instruments for the latent factors (Jöreskog & Sörbom, 1984, p. I.37). It is computed as

$$\text{Coeff. of Det.} = 1 - |\underset{\sim}{\Theta}| \, / \, |\underset{\sim}{S}|$$

where $|\underset{\sim}{\Theta}|$ is the determinant of the covariance matrix of the measurement errors and $|\underset{\sim}{S}|$ is the determinant of the covariance matrix of the observed variables. This figure is routinely reported in the LISREL output.

The validity of a measurement model indicates the average variance extracted for the construct(s), and is calculated as follows[7] (Dillon & Goldstein, 1984, p. 480):

$$\text{Validity} = \frac{\sum_{i=1}^{p} \lambda_{yi}^2}{\sum_{i=1}^{p} \lambda_{yi}^2 + \sum_{i=1}^{p} \text{var}(e_{yi})}$$

where λ_{yi} is the standardized factor loading for Y_i, $\text{var}(e_{yi})$ is the error variance of Y_i. Because the LISREL output does not report this figure, it has to be computed by hand. The resulting reliabilities and validities are reported in Table 15.

Table 15
Reliabilities of and Validities of CFA Models

| | Group | | | | | |
	Asian		Hispanic		Anglo	
	Exogenous Variables[a]					
	Rel.	Val.	Rel.	Val.	Rel.	Val.
Simple	.924	.435	.887	.361	.689	.542
Modified	.937	.452	.887	.298	·	·
	Endogenous Variables[b]					
	Rel.	Val.	Rel.	Val.	Rel.	Val.
Simple	.999	.530	.956	.415	.991	.475
Modified	.994	.577	.989	.516	.978	.492

[a] The reliability and validity of the measurement model for the Anglo group are for the SES only.

[b] The reliabilities and validities of Model 1 for the Asian and Hispanic groups were calculated from the TSLS estimates.

The reliabilities of the measurement models turned out to be very satisfactory—most of them were in the range of .888 to .991. The reliability of the initial simple model for the Anglo group (.689) was lower than that of the others primarily because only one construct (SES) was included in the measurement model.

The validities of the measurement models are less encouraging. They ranged from .298 to .577, with the majority falling in the neighborhood of .50. The validities of the measurement models for the exogenous variables were particularly low for the Hispanic (.361 for the simple model and .298 for the modified model). As suggested by Dillon and Goldstein (1984), a validity index of .50 or above is generally considered acceptable. Therefore the validities of the measurement models demonstrated a marginally acceptable level.

The resulting parameter estimates from the above confirmatory factor analyses are graphically presented in Figure 6.

Figure 6. Parameter estimates of CFA measurement models.

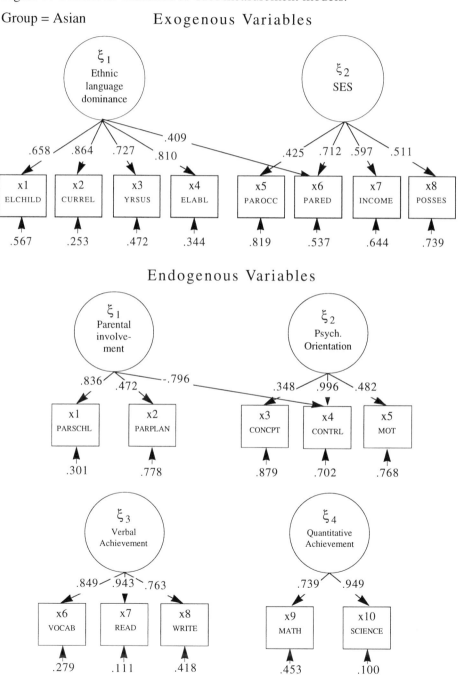

Figure 6. (Continued from previous page)

Group = Hispanic   Exogenous Variables

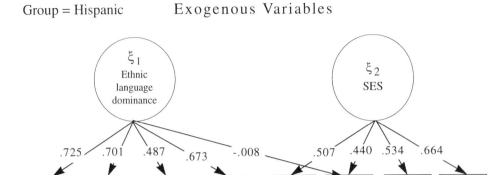

Endogenous Variables

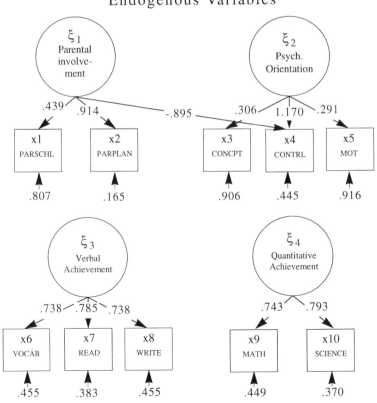

Figure 6. (Continued from previous page.)

Group = Anglo

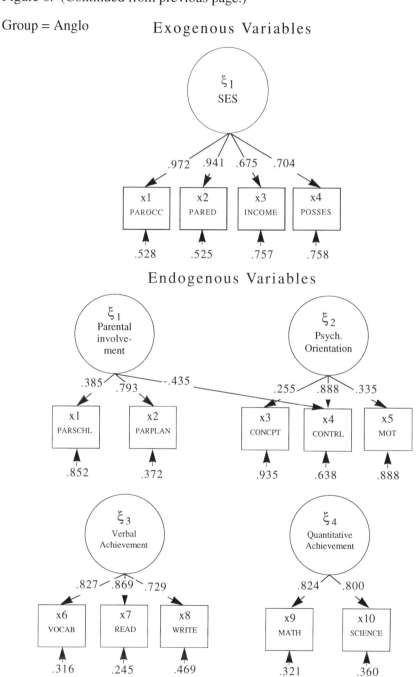

Exogenous Variables

Endogenous Variables

Covariance Structure Analysis

Single-Group Covariance Structure Analysis

After a satisfactory level of reliability and validity of the measurement models had been demonstrated, single-group covariance structure analyses followed, which estimated, among other things, the structural coefficients indicating the causal links among the six latent constructs.

It can be recalled that the structural covariance models to be tested were underidentified (see the section on Analyses in Chapter Two). This underidentification created special difficulties in the parameter estimation. The strategy adopted was to subject the initial underidentified model to LISREL analyses and use the resulting parameter estimates as input to the subsequent runs. By having fewer parameters to estimate and by setting one of the reciprocal paths to a fixed value, the model became identified.

Two parameters were chosen in the effort to make the model identified: BE(4,2), which is the path from verbal achievement to psychological orientation, and BE(4,3), which is the path from quantitative achievement to psychological orientation. By fixing the two paths to some pre-determined values, the estimation of parameters representing simultaneous causality was eliminated, and thus the model became identified. The process of searching for an optimal-fitting covariance structure model for each of the three ethnic groups is summarized in Table 16.

Starting with the Asian group, the initial model as described in Chapter One yielded less-than-satisfactory fit statistics. The chi-square value was significant at $p < .000$, the GFI was .830, and the RMSR was .089. The χ^2/df ratio was, however, a quite decent 1.921.

Because the model was underidentified, some of the resulting modification indices were invalid, e.g., negative. Fortunately, the confirmatory factor analyses described in the preceding section already suggested a complex loading of parental education on both SES and ethnic-language dominance. The results of the modified model after freeing the factor loading LX(6,1) are presented as Model 2 in Table 16.

Table 16
Specification Search in Single-Group Covariance
Structure Analysis

Model	χ^2	df	p	GFI	Adj. GFI	RMSR	χ^2/df
			Asian				
1. Initial	226.63	118	.000	.830	.754	.089	1.921
2. LX(6,1)	212.88	117	.000	.839	.764	.081	1.819
3. BE(4,2)=0, BE(4,3)=.353	212.88	119	.000	.840	.768	.081	1.789
			Hispanic				
1. Initial	192.37	118	.000	.921	.885	.059	1.630
2. LY(9,1)	175.74	117	.000	.926	.892	.053	1.502
3. BE(4,2)= BE(4,3)=0	175.74	119	.001	.926	.894	.053	1.477
			Anglo				
1. Initial [a]	—	—	—	—	—	—	—
2. LY(9,1)	143.99	65	.000	.949	.918	.049	2.215
3. BE(4,2)=0, BE(4,3)=.289	131.63	67	.000	.954	.928	.045	1.965

[a] The parameters in the initial model for the Anglo group, with or without freeing BE(3,2), was unestimatable.

Although the chi-square difference (226.63 - 212.88 = 13.75) was highly significant at an alpha level of even .001, indicating a significant fit improvement from freeing this parameter, the lack-of-fit chi-square was still significant with p < .000, and the increase in the GFI was only negligible (from .830 to .839). The decrease in the χ^2/df ratio was not impressive either, dropping only from 1.921 to 1.819. However, since the overall fit was already at an acceptable level, the decision was to stop refining the measurement model component of the covariance structure model.

Model 2, however, was still underidentified. Using the parameter estimates in Model 2, BE(4,2) was fixed to 0 and BE(4,3) to .353; the model thus became identified. This identified model had almost exactly the same fit statistics, as evident in Table 16. The χ^2/df ratio of 1.789 indicates that the fit of the final model was reasonable. Other indices also indicate acceptable fit, with GFI of .840 and RMSR of .081.

Exactly the same procedure was followed in estimating the Hispanic model. The initial model had a better fit than that of the Asian group. Although the lack-of-fit was again significant with p < .000, the GFI was a solid .921, the RMSR was under .06, and the χ^2/df ratio was a decent 1.630. Because allowing a complex loading for parental education did not significantly improve the CFA model fit for the Hispanic, instead allowing internal locus of control to load on both psychological orientation and parental involvement did, it was decided to free LY(9,1), which is the loading of internal locus of control on parental involvement. The resulting model, Model 2, was a significant improvement over Model 1 (chi-difference was 16.63), but the lack-of-fit statistic was still significant at p < .000. Because the resulting χ^2/df ratio of 1.502 can be generally considered satisfactory fit, the specification search for a better-fitting measurement model stopped.

Both BE(4,2) and BE(4,3) of Model 2 for the Hispanic group were very close to zero (-.008 for BE(4,2) and .047 for BE(4,3)). They were therefore fixed to zero and the model was re-estimated. The final fit statistics were almost identical to those of Model 2, except that the p-value was raised to .001. The χ^2/df ratio was a very decent 1.477, so was the GFI (.926) and RMSR (.053).

Estimation of the covariance structure model for the Anglo group presented even more difficulties. Recalling that the zero-order correlations between verbal and quantitative achievement measures were quite high for the Anglo group, it was decided to revise the initial model by adding a causal path from verbal to quantitative achievement, i.e., BE(3,2). However, for reasons still baffling the author at the time of the writing, the programs for estimating this initial model, with or without freeing BE(3,2), failed completely. In light of the error message "Serious problems were encountered during minimization. Either the model is inconsistent with data or the arithmetic precision is insufficient," the only explanation would be that the zero-order correlations provide misleading information about the causal relationship between verbal and quantitative achievement. It was thus decided to delete this causal path from verbal to quantitative achievement.

Again, the modification indices were not helpful because of the underidentification problem. The only clue for model modification was the significant complex loading of internal locus of control on parental involvement in the CFA model in Table 12. I thus experimented with freeing LY(9,1), as was done for the Hispanic group.

The results were finally comprehensible, and even quite encouraging. The fit statistics were even better than those of the Asian and Hispanic groups. The lack-of-fit was still significant (p < .000), but the GFI was very high—.949. Even the RMSR dropped below .05. The χ^2/df ratio, however, was over 2.0, larger than that of the Asian and Hispanic groups.

Using the results of Model 2 estimation, BE(4,2) was fixed to zero and BE(4,3) was fixed at .289. The model was then re-estimated. The final identified model yielded very good fit. The improvement of fit was highly significant (chi-difference = 143.99 − 131.63 = 12.36), although the lack-of-fit chi-square value was still high (p < .000). But the GFI increased to .954, the RMSR dropped even further to .045, and the χ^2/df became a nice 1.965.

After the fit has been demonstrated as acceptable, we now turn to the parameter estimates of the single-group covariance structure model for each group presented in Table 17. Besides the parameter estimates themselves, the standard errors which accompanied the ML method are also reported in Table 17 as parenthetical values. In addition, those parameter estimates whose t-values (defined as the parameter estimate divided by its standard error) are greater than 2 are marked with an asterisk, indicating a parameter significantly different from zero at alpha = .05.

Proceeding first with the lambda Y values, or the factor loadings of endogenous variables, we see that most of the loadings were significant. The first loading of every latent endogenous factor was fixed at one so as to assign the unit of measurement of the observed endogenous variable to the latent endogenous factor (Jöreskog & Sörbom, 1984, p. I.7). As a result, no parameter estimates were produced for those fixed values, and

Table 17
Parameter Estimates of Single-Group Covariance Structure Model

LAMBDA Y (Factor Loadings of Endogenous Variables)

	Asian				Hispanic				Anglo			
	η_1	η_2	η_3	η_4	η_1	η_2	η_3	η_4	η_1	η_2	η_3	η_4
PARSCHL	1.000	0	0	0	1.000	0	0	0	1.000	0	0	0
PARPLAN	.562*	0	0	0	1.115*	0	0	0	1.727*	0	0	0
	(.243)				(.240)				(.356)			
VOCAB	0	1.000	0	0	0	1.000	0	0	0	1.000	0	0
READING	0	1.080*	0	0	0	1.047*	0	0	0	1.048*	0	0
		(.079)				(.088)				(.054)		
WRITING	0	.882*	0	0	0	.993*	0	0	0	.876*	0	0
		(.089)				(.088)				(.057)		
MATH	0	0	1.000	0	0	0	1.000	0	0	0	1.000	0
SCIENCE	0	0	1.252*	0	0	0	1.054*	0	0	0	.973*	0
			(.132)				(.087)				(.058)	
CONCPT	0	0	0	1.000	0	0	0	1.000	0	0	0	1.000
CONTRL	0	0	0	1.499*	-1.615	0	0	3.380	-.916	0	0	2.683*
				(.456)	(.950)			(1.800)	(.523)			(.771)
MOT	0	0	0	.996*	0	0	0	.844*	0	0	0	1.133*
				(.375)				(.284)				(.295)

LAMBDA X (Factor Loadings of Exogenous Variables)

	ξ_1	ξ_2	ξ_1	ξ_2	ξ_1
ELCHILD	.653*	0	.714*	0	
	(.087)		(.064)		
CURREL	.851*	0	.718*	0	
	(.079)		(.064)		
YRSUS	.739*	0	.477*	0	
	(.084)		(.068)		
ELABL	.816*	0	.673*	0	
	(.081)		(.065)		
PAROCC	0	.404*	0	.534*	1.000
		(.107)		(.073)	
PARED	.399*	.682*	0	.475*	.957*
	(.117)	(.124)		(.073)	(.103)
INCOME	0	.595*	0	.520*	.685*
		(.104)		(.073)	(.093)
POSSESS	0	.558*	0	.632*	.778*
		(.104)		(.073)	(.096)

Table 17 (continued)

	Asian	Hispanic	Anglo

BETA (Structural Coefficients among Endogenous Factors)

	η_1	η_2	η_3	η_4	η_1	η_2	η_3	η_4	η_1	η_2	η_3	η_4
η_1	0	0	0	0	0	0	0	0	0	0	0	0
η_2	-.412	0	0	2.462	-.751*	0	0	1.564*	-2.422*	0	0	3.384*
	(1.644)			(10.642)	(.353)			(.612)	(.801)			(1.087)
η_3	-.502	-.103	0	2.289	.120	1.015*	0	-.223	-2.205	0	0	3.425
	(2.643)	(2.692)		(16.453)	(.184)	(.108)		(.312)	(1.553)			(2.658)
η_4	.204	0	.353	0	.445*	0	0	0	.643*	0	.289	0
	(.105)				(.142)				(.176)			

GAMMA (Structural Coefficients from Exogenous to Endogenous Factors)

	ξ_1	ξ_2	ξ_1	ξ_2	ξ_1
η_1	.126	.160	.088	.349*	.333*
	(.109)	(.123)	(.068)	(.084)	(.077)
η_2	-.258	-.060	-.160*	.150	.632*
	(.138)	(1.939)	(.077)	(.105)	(.184)
η_3	-.080	-.040	.166*	.099	.619*
	(.719)	(2.088)	(.059)	(.080)	(.172)
η_4	.019	.064	.033	.039	-.179*
	(.053)	(.075)	(.031)	(.043)	(.049)

PHI (Correlations Among Exogenous Factors)

	ξ_1	ξ_2	ξ_1	ξ_2
ξ_1	1.000		1.000	
ξ_2	-.361*	1.000	-.438*	1.000
	(.124)		(.081)	

THETA EPS (Measurement Errors of Endogenous Variables) and Squared Multiple Correlations (Reliabilities)

	Error	Rel.	Error	Rel.	Error	Rel.
PARSCHL	.277	.723	.643	.357	.829	.171
PARPLAN	.772	.228	.556	.444	.489	.511
VOCAB	.257	.743	.436	.564	.313	.687
READING	.133	.867	.382	.618	.245	.755
WRITING	.421	.597	.445	.555	.472	.528
MATH	.440	.560	.423	.577	.328	.672
SCIENCE	.122	.878	.350	.650	.369	.631
CONCPT	.877	.123	.874	.126	.928	.072
CONTRL	.742	.258	.465	.535	.709	.291
MOT	.878	.122	.910	.090	.884	.116

Table 17 (continued)

	Asian		Hispanic		Anglo	

THETA DELTA (Measurement Errors of Exogenous Variables)
and Squared Multiple Correlations (Reliabilities)

	Errror	Rel.	Errror	Rel.		
ELCHILD	.574	.426	.490	.510		
CURREL	.275	.725	.484	.516		
YRSUS	.454	.546	.773	.227		
ELABL	.333	.667	.547	.453		
PAROCC	.837	.163	.715	.285	.524	.476
PARED	.573	.427	.774	.226	.564	.436
INCOME	.645	.355	.729	.271	.777	.223
POSSESS	.689	.311	.601	.399	.712	.288

Squared Multiple Correlations and Residuals for Structural Equations

	SMC	Res.	SMC	Res.	SMC	Res.
η_1	.037	.696	.288	.254	.309	.118
η_2	.826	.129	.321	.383	.890	.075
η_3	.960	.023	.949	.030	.999	.001
η_4	.981	.002	.640	.046	1.000	.000

Total Coefficient of Determination

Endog. Var.	.991		.976	.968
Exogen. Var.	.934		.886	.681
Str. Equ.	.981		.644	.702

Note. Values in parentheses are standard errors.

* $p < .05$.

therefore no standard errors or t-values were calculated. Note also that some loadings, despite their large absolute values, were not significant because of large standard errors.

In estimating the lambda X values, or the factor loadings of the exogenous variables, a different approach was adopted for the Asian and Hispanic groups. Instead of fixing the first loading of every latent exogenous factor to one, the latent exogenous factors were standardized so that their variances were scaled to unity. This has the same effect as assigning the unit of measurement of the observed exogenous variable to the latent exogenous factor. The resulting parameter estimates were all significantly different from zero.

The second part of Table 17 captures the essence of this study—the causal links among the latent factors. Note that the following presentation of the causal linkage among the latent factors pertains to the direct effects only. Discussion on the total effects (direct effects plus indirect effects) can be found in Chapter Four.

The beta matrix contains the structural coefficients among the endogenous factors. The effect of parental involvement (η_1) on academic achievement (η_2 and η_3) appears to be mostly negative—quite contrary to the popular notion that parental involvement fosters achievement growth. This is particularly evident for the Hispanic and Anglo groups on verbal achievement (-.751 for the Hispanic and -2.422 for the Anglo). The only exception is BE(3,1) for the Hispanic, which indicates a small and nonsignificant positive effect of parental involvement on quantitative achievement (.120). On the other hand, parental involvement brought about positive change in psychological orientation (η_4), as the BE(4,1) values were uniformly positive, but only significant for the Hispanic (.445) and Anglo (.643) groups.

One of the most interesting findings of this study is the differential effect of verbal achievement (η_2) on quantitative achievement (η_3) among groups. For the Asian group, this effect was nonsignificantly negative (-.103); for the Hispanic group, this effect was strongly positive (1.105); for the Anglo, this effect was fixed at zero.

Turning now to the causal relationship between psychological orientation and academic achievement, we can see that the effect of verbal achievement on psychological orientation (BE(4,2)) was largely absent—it was found to be zero for all three groups. It was fixed to zero after the preliminary runs indicated it was close to zero. The effect of quantitative achievement on psychological orientation was mildly positive for the Asian (.353) and Anglo (.289), and zero for the Hispanic.

The effect of psychological orientation on academic achievement, on the other hand, tended to be strongly positive. The effect was particularly stronger for the verbal achievement (2.462 for the Asian, 1.564 for the Hispanic, and 3.384 for the

Anglo) than quantitative achievement (2.289 for the Asian, -.223 for the Hispanic, and 3.425 for the Anglo).

The gamma matrix contains the structural coefficients from the exogenous factors to the endogenous factors. Ethnic-language dominance had a small and positive, but nonsignificant, effect on parental involvement (.126 for the Asian and .088 for the Hispanic). This suggests that especially for the Asian group, parents whose children were ethnic-language dominant tended to be more involved in their children's academic study.

One of the major findings of this study is the negative effect of ethnic-language dominance on verbal achievement (η_2). For the Asian group, this effect was a moderate negative -.258, although not quite significant because of the relatively large standard error (.138). In fact, this is the only effect in the gamma matrix for the Asian group that was close to being statistically significant. This effect was smaller for the Hispanic in magnitude (-.160), but because of smaller standard error (.077), it was statistically significant. This finding provides partial evidence that ethnic-language dominance had an undesirable effect on language minority students' verbal achievement.

Another interesting finding is the effect of ethnic-language dominance on quantitative achievement (η_3). For the Asian group, the effect was a very small negative value (-.080); whereas for the Hispanic group, the effect was a significantly positive .166. This provides partial support to the assertion that linguistic and cognitive development in the ethnic language helps promote quantitative achievement, once partialling out the intermediate effect of verbal achievement in the English language. However, this seems to hold true only for the Hispanic. Ethnic-language dominance does not seem to play a role in Asian students' quantitative learning.

Lastly, the effect of ethnic-language dominance on psychological orientation (η_4) was virtually nonexistent: .019 for the Asian and .033 for the Hispanic. This probably contradicts with the claim of ethnic language advocates that ethnic identity preserved through the ethnic language promotes healthy psychological growth. No evidence was found to link the two.

Next we turn to the effect of SES (ξ_2) on the four endogenous factors (η_1, η_2, η_3, and η_4). Not surprisingly, we found uniformly positive effects of SES on parental involvement (η_1) for all three groups (.160 for the Asian, .349 for the Hispanic, and .333 for the Anglo), although the effect was not significant for the Asian group. This suggests that higher socio-economic status provided the incentives for the parents to be more involved in their children's academic study.

The direct effect of SES on academic achievement varied quite dramatically among groups. It exerted a very slight negative effect on both verbal and quantitative achievements for the Asian group (-.060 and -.040), a small and positive effect for the Hispanic (.150 and .099), but a very large positive effect for the Anglo (.632 and .619). There was no evidence that SES would affect verbal and quantitative achievements differentially, however. Lastly, the effects of SES on psychological orientation were negligible for the Asian (.064) and Hispanic (.0389), but was significantly negative for the Anglo group (-.179). The finding of a negative effect for the Anglo group invites some challenge in theoretical justification since it contradicts the common theory that socio-economically better-off students tend to have more positive thinking about themselves and about schooling.

Before moving on to model evaluation, there is another set of parameter estimates of interest—the phi matrix which contains the correlations among the latent exogenous factors. For both the Asian and Hispanic groups, ethnic-language dominance (ξ_1) and SES (ξ_2) were found to be negatively correlated. The magnitude of this correlation was somewhat higher for the Hispanic (-.438) than for the Asian (-.361). Both correlations were significant in both practical and statistical sense.

Having presented the results of the parameter estimates of the factor loadings and structural coefficients, it is time that we evaluate the model from various angles. The results of model evaluation are presented in the last part of Table 17.

First, we examine the errors of measurement and their corresponding reliabilities of the indicator variables. The THETA EPS matrix contains the errors of measurement of the observed endogenous variables. For ease of presentation, their corresponding squared multiple correlations, or reliabilities are presented right alongside the measurement errors. It is clear that the reliabilities varied tremendously among the variables both within and across groups. For the Asian group, the reliabilities ranged from .122 to .878, with a mean reliability of .510. For the Hispanic group, the reliabilities ranged from .090 to .650, with a mean of .452. For the Anglo group, the reliabilities ranged from .072 to .755, with a mean of .443. In general, the measures of psychological orientation had the poorest reliabilities, particularly with self-concept and motivation.

The THETA DELTA matrix contains the errors of measurement of the observed exogenous variables. Their corresponding reliabilities show that they are not much better than those of the endogenous variables. For the Asian group, the reliabilities varied from .163 to .725, with a mean of .453. For the Hispanic group, they varied from .226 to .516, with a mean of .361. For the Anglo group, they varied from .223 to .476, with a mean of .356. As with the endogenous variables, the reliabilities were generally higher for the Asian and lower for the Anglo.

The squared multiple correlation (SMC) for the ith structural equation is defined

$$SMC = 1 - Var(\zeta_i) / Var(\eta_i)$$

where $Var(\zeta_i)$ is the error variance (residual) of the ith structural equation and $Var(\eta_i)$ is the variance of the ith latent endogenous variable. It is interpreted as the proportion of the variance in each latent endogenous variable explained by its precedent latent variable(s).

Naturally, the SMC's turned out to be smallest for the 1st structural equation (η_1) for all three groups because, in the case of the Asian and Hispanic groups, only two latent variables (ethnic-language dominance and SES) were used to explain the variance of parental involvement, and in the case of the Anglo group, only one (SES). The more latent variables entered the structural equation as the explanatory factors, the more likely that the explained proportion would be larger, as was clearly the trend from η_1 to η_4. Note that η_4 of the Hispanic group was smaller than η_2 and η_3 because η_2 and η_3, which were assumed to be causal factors of η_4, turned out to have no effect on η_4.

As it turned out, ethnic-language dominance and SES explained virtually none of the variance of parental involvement for the Asian group (.037); whereas they explained about a quarter of the variance for the Hispanic (.288) and SES alone explained more than 30% for Anglo (.309) group. This finding probably suggests that for the Asian parents, their involvement in their children's academic study was independent of either SES or ethnic language status.

As for the second structural equation, verbal achievement was very well explained by ethnic-language dominance, SES, and parental involvement for the Asian group (.826) and rather poorly explained for the Hispanic (.321). For the Anglo group, SES and parental involvement alone explained almost 90% (.890) of the variance.

Turning now to the third structural equation, or quantitative achievement, the proportion explained was uniformly very high for all three groups (.960 for the Asian, .949 for the Hispanic, and .999 for the Anglo). This indicates that variance in quantitative achievement was very well captured by ethnic-language dominance, SES, and verbal achievement.

The last structural equation was psychological orientation. The proportion explained was .981 for the Asian group, .640 for the Hispanic, and a perfect 1.000 for the Anglo! A zero residual seems quite unlikely in practice, and therefore may need to be examined with caution.

As a last measure of model evaluation, the coefficients of determination were calculated. They are defined as

$$1 - |\underset{\sim}{\Psi}| \ / \ |\text{Cov}(\eta)|,$$

where $|\underset{\sim}{\Psi}|$ is the determinant of the PSI matrix and $|\text{Cov}(\eta)|$ is the determinant of the covariance matrix of the η's. It is indicative of how well the variables of interest were explained jointly by their antecedent variables.

The LISREL output produced three coefficients of determination: the endogenous variables, the exogenous variables, and the structural equations. They are reported in the bottom of the last part of Table 17. Here we see that the coefficients of determination were very high for the endogenous variables

(.991 for the Asian, .976 for the Hispanic, and .968 for the Anglo). For the exogenous variables, the coefficients of determination were still very good for the Asian (.934) and Hispanic (.886), but dropped to .681 for the Anglo. Lastly, the coefficients of determination for the structural equations still held strong for the Asian (.981), but weakened for the Hispanic (.644) and the Anglo (.702).

A graphical representation of the parameter estimates of the single-group covariance structural models are presented in Figure 7.

Multi-Group Covariance Structure Analysis

Multi-group covariance structure analysis simultaneously estimates parameters for several groups with some or all of them constrained to be equal across groups. This procedure provides at least two advantages: (a) it allows for significance testing of the equality constraints, and (b) it allows for efficient estimation of the parameters.

The fitting function to minimize during multi-group covariance structure analysis is

$$F = \sum_{g=1}^{G} (N_g / N) \, F_g \, (\underset{\sim}{\Sigma}_g, \underset{\sim}{S}_g) ,$$

where the subscript g denotes the gth group and for ML method

$$F_g = \log |\underset{\sim}{\Sigma}_g| + \mathrm{tr}(\underset{\sim}{S}_g \underset{\sim}{\Sigma}_g^{-1}) - \log |\underset{\sim}{S}_g| - (p + q)$$

where p is the number of observed endogenous variables and q is the number of observed exogenous variables.

Several decisions were made before proceeding with the multi-group analysis:

1. In order to test the equality of several covariance structure models, it must first be demonstrated that their measurement models are equal. If the measurement models are found to be variant, there is no need to pursue further.

2. Because the measurement models of the three groups involve different sets of both latent and observed variables, this

Figure 7. Parameter estimates of single-group covariance structure model.
Group = Asian

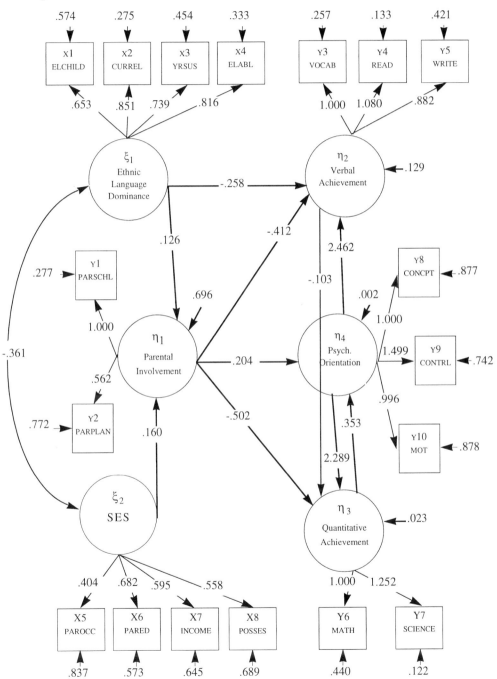

Note: The loading of X_6 on ξ_1 (not shown) is .399.

Figure 7. (Continued from previous page)
Group = Hispanic

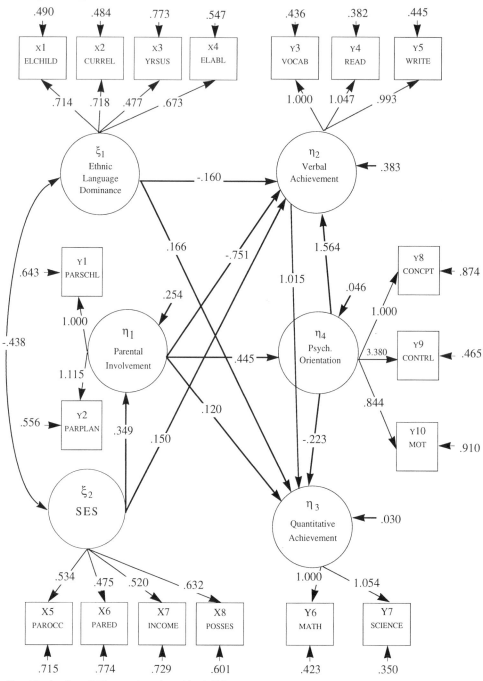

Note: The loading of Y9 on η_1 (not shown) is -1.615.

Figure 7. (Continued from previous page)

Group = Anglo

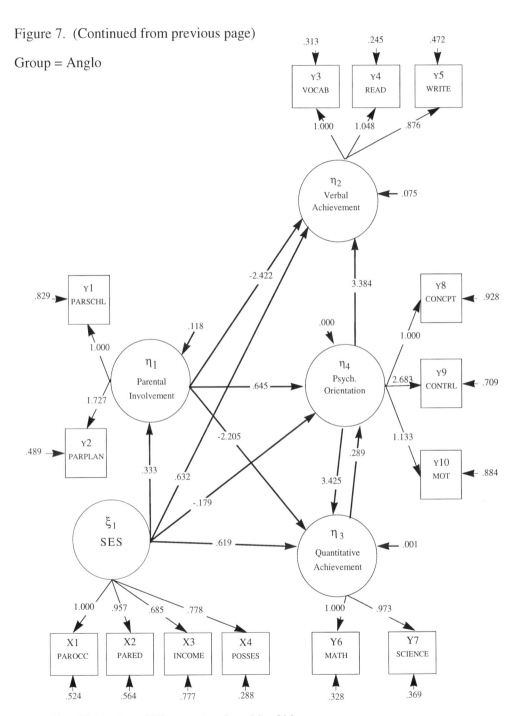

Note: The loading of Y9 on η_1 (not shown) is -.916.

invariance test cannot be carried out for all three groups simultaneously. Instead, only two groups can be tested at one time.

3. The input matrix used for testing the invariance hypotheses should be the covariance matrix rather than the correlation matrix because the latter statistically removes the differences in variability among groups by standardization, which tends to obscure the distinction between the true parameters in the populations (Duncan, 1975).

In testing the invariance of two measurement models, five equality constraints were tested in a hierarchical order; i.e, each subsequent test of equality presupposed the preceding tests of equality. First, LX = PS, or no equality constraint. The hypothesis being tested was a simple model with no equality constraints. This was used as the baseline for comparison upon which the subsequent equality constraints were tested for significance in fit deterioration. Next, LX = IN, or invariance of factor loadings between groups. If the chi-square increase was significant, the factor loadings would be judged as not equal. Third, LX = IN and TD = IN, or invariance of factor loadings and measurement errors. If the chi-square increase was significant, but the previous chi-square increase was not, then the two models would be judged as invariant in their factor loadings but not measurement errors. Fourth, LX = IN, TD = IN, and PH = IN, or invariance of factor loadings, measurement errors, and inter-factor correlations. This tested the additional equality constraint that the inter-factor correlation matrices were invariant. Lastly, $\Sigma_1 = \Sigma_2$, or invariance of variance-covariance matrices. This was the strongest form of equality constraint, testing the hypothesis that all parameters in the two models were invariant.

The results of the multi-group covariance structure analysis testing the equality of measurement models are summarized in Table 18.

A quick glance at Table 18 is all it takes to conclude that the measurement models for the exogenous variables among the three groups were not equal. For the Hispanic vs. Asian comparison, the equality test failed at Hypothesis 2, or the invariance of the factor loadings. The chi-square difference was 42.79, and the df difference was 9, significant at p < .001. For

Table 18
Multi-Group Covariance Structure Analysis-Invariance of Measurement Models

Hypothesis	χ^2	df	p	GFI	RMSR	Decision
Exogenous Variables						
Hispanic vs. Asian						
1. Simple	81.74	36	.000	.925	4.140	—
2. Lambdas	124.53	45	.000	.887	9.587	Reject
3. Lambdas, Errors	163.60	53	.000	.849	20.945	Reject
4. Lambdas, Errors, Phi	168.59	54	.000	.845	20.720	Reject
5. Sigma	113.72	36	.000	.877	20.419	Reject
Anglo vs. Hispanic						
1. Simple	31.77	2	.000	.985	4.846	—
2. Lambdas	45.11	6	.000	.966	7.889	Reject
3. Lambdas, Errors	79.48	10	.000	.934	11.137	Reject
4. Lambdas, Errors, Phi	82.34	11	.000	.933	21.585	Reject
5. Sigma	50.62	10	.000	.944	18.446	Reject
Anglo vs. Asian						
1. Simple	27.68	2	.000	.988	5.256	—
2. Lambdas	34.46	6	.000	.963	20.284	Accept
3. Lambdas, Errors	−9400.66	10	1.000	.000	466.170	Reject
4. Lambdas, Errors, Phi	1743.52	11	.000	.416	60.495	Reject
5. Sigma	36.94	10	.000	.951	58.220	Reject
Endogenous Variables						
Hispanic vs. Asian						
1. Simple	74.53	54	.033	.922	0.565	—
2. Lambdas	103.71	66	.002	.899	2.245	Reject
3. Lambdas, Errors	124.49	76	.000	.879	2.514	Reject
4. Lambdas, Errors, Phi	137.85	82	.000	.867	2.504	Reject
5. Sigma	104.14	55	.000	.897	2.495	Reject
Anglo vs. Hispanic						
1. Simple	59.84	54	.272	.982	0.193	—
2. Lambdas	80.20	66	.112	.978	0.924	Accept
3. Lambdas, Errors	98.61	76	.042	.974	0.904	Accept
4. Lambdas, Errors, Phi	116.09	82	.008	.970	0.907	Reject
5. Sigma	75.65	55	.034	.983	0.895	Reject
Anglo vs. Asian						
1. Simple	82.98	54	.007	.922	.565	—
2. Lambdas	104.97	66	.002	.897	1.413	Accept
3. Lambdas, Errors	132.03	76	.000	.867	1.569	Reject
4. Lambdas, Errors, Phi	139.01	82	.000	.863	1.514	Reject
5. Sigma	81.69	55	.011	.907	1.486	Reject

Note. The significance level for rejection is .01. Comparisons of the measurement models for the exogenous variables involving the Anglo group are for the SES construct only.

the Anglo vs. Hispanic comparison, the equality test also failed at Hypothesis 2, with a chi-square difference of 31.74 and df difference of 4, also significant at p < .001.

For the Anglo vs. Asian comparison, the equality test failed at Hypothesis 3, which yielded incomprehensible results because of serious model-data misfit. Therefore the decision to reject this hypothesis should be well justified.

Much the same can be said about the results of the measurement models for the endogenous variables in the second part of Table 18. The measurement models for the endogenous variables were clearly unequal among the three groups, but the rejection of the equality hypothesis occurred somewhat later in the hierarchical level. For the Hispanic vs. Asian comparison, the equality test failed at Hypothesis 2 (chi-square difference = 29.18, df difference = 12, significant at p < .01), meaning that the two measurement models differed fundamentally in their factor loadings.

The Anglo and Hispanic groups were more alike in their measurement models of the endogenous variables than those of the exogenous variables. The equality test failed at Hypothesis 4, with a chi-square difference of 17.48 and a df difference of 6, significant at p < .01. This means that the Anglo and Hispanic groups were similar to each other in their factor loadings and even measurement errors, but the inter-factor correlations were not the same. The Anglo vs. Asian comparison was much the same as that for the exogenous variables. The equality test failed at Hypothesis 3, with a chi-square difference of 27.06 and a df difference of 10, significant at p < .01. This means that the Anglo and the Asian groups had similar factor loadings, but their measurement errors varied significantly.

In sum, all three groups were found to differ from each other in their measurement models of either the exogenous or endogenous variables. The Asian and Hispanic groups were most dissimiliar since not even their factor loadings were the same. The Anglo and the Asian groups were invariant in their factor loadings, but not so in their measurement errors. The Anglo and Hispanic groups were very dissimilar in their factor loadings of the exogenous variables but they only differed in the inter-factor correlations for the endogenous variables.

Pooled-Sample Covariance Structure Analysis

The last part of the analytical procedures in this study is pooled-sample covariance structure analysis which examined the effect of ethnicity on the six latent constructs. The pooled-sample consisted of the Asian and Hispanic groups only because they were the two language minority groups of primary interest in this study and because they both involved all of the six latent constructs.

This set of analyses differed from the previous single-sample and multi-sample covariance structure analyses in two important ways:

1. Because group membership was coded as a dichotomous variable in the model, a special control card "MV=2" was specified in the LISREL program to compute the polyserial correlations instead of the usual product moment correlations, which were then used as the input to the LISREL runs.

2. Because the resulting input correlation matrix turned out to be non-positive definite, the ULS (unweighted least squares) method instead of the ML method was used. It has been shown that when the number of Y variables is large, the ULS method serves as a satisfactory compromise for a more precise but less feasible treatment proposed by Muthen (1981).

Before presenting the results of the pooled-sample analysis, a cautionary note is in order. First, since the preceding analyses have demonstrated the incomparability between the Asian and Hispanic groups, sample pooling may not be empirically justifiable. Second, since different estimation methods were used in the single-group analysis (i.e., ML method) and pooled-sample analysis (i.e., ULS method), direct comparison between the resulting estimates from the two analyses should be avoided.

Based on the above consideration, the sole utility of the pooled-sample covariance structure analysis would be to illustrate the strong ethnicity effect on the six latent constructs. Substantive interpretation of the structural coefficients among the six latent constructs is consequently not advisable.

The initial model as presented in Chapter One yielded less-than-acceptable results: the GFI was .854, the adjusted GFI was .787, and the RMSE was .083. The only modification index large enough to suggest a change that was both theoretically and empirically justifiable was LY(3,2), or the factor loading of YRSUS on SES. In other words, the length of residence in the U.S. might be claimed to be a direct indicator of socio-economic status.

The model was revised accordingly and the parameters were re-estimated. The modified model represents a substantial improvement over the initial one, with a GFI of .968, adjusted GFI of .953, and RMSR of .062. Recall, however, that this model was still underidentified because of the simultaneous causality between academic achievement and psychological orientation. In order to remove the reciprocal paths between verbal achievement and psychological orientation (BE(6,4)) and between quantitative achievement and psychological orientation (BE(6,5)), these two parameters were fixed at 1.367 and -1.089 respectively, using the results from the previous LISREL run. The model was then re-estimated. The results are presented in Table 19.

The loadings of the altogether eighteen endogenous variables on their respective latent constructs were all consistently high, including the freed parameter LY(3,2), which had a loading of 1.011. This indicates that length of residence in the U.S. measured not only ethnic-language dominance but also socio-economic status. The loading of the single exogenous variable was set at 1.000 to indicate that there was only one indicator variable for group membership. Accordingly, its associated measurement error (TD(1,1)) was set as zero to indicate no measurement error as a result of the designation.

The beta matrix contains the direct effects of the six latent constructs on each other. They indicate the net effects of these latent constructs without the contamination of difference in ethnicity.

Starting with ethnic-language dominance (η_1), we can see that it affected SES negatively (-.316), even after partialing out the ethnicity effect. On parental involvement, being ethnic-language dominant still means that the parents monitored their children closely (.436). Ethnic-language dominance also tended to cause deficiencies in the English language (-.466). However, ethnic language did appear to facilitate quantitative processing

Table 19
Parameter Estimates of Pooled-Sample Covariance
Structure Model

LAMBDA Y (Factor Loadings of Endogenous Variables)

	η_1	η_2	η_3	η_4	η_5	η_6
ELCHILD	1.000	0	0	0	0	0
CURREL	1.666	0	0	0	0	0
YRSUS	1.360	1.011	0	0	0	0
ELABL	1.438	0	0	0	0	0
PAROCC	0	1.000	0	0	0	0
PARED	0	.970	0	0	0	0
INCOME	0	1.012	0	0	0	0
POSSESS	0	1.142	0	0	0	0
PARSCHL	0	0	1.000	0	0	0
PARPLAN	0	0	1.760	0	0	0
VOCAB	0	0	0	1.000	0	0
READING	0	0	0	1.033	0	0
WRITING	0	0	0	1.062	0	0
MATH	0	0	0	0	1.000	0
SCIENCE	0	0	0	0	.981	0
CONCPT	0	0	0	0	0	1.000
CONTRL	0	0	0	0	0	1.412
MOT	0	0	0	0	0	.839

LAMBDA X (Factor Loadings of Exogenous Variables)

	ξ_1
GROUP	1.000

BETA (Structual Coefficients among Endogenous Variables)

	η_1	η_2	η_3	η_4	η_5	η_6
η_1	0	0	0	0	0	0
η_2	-.316	0	0	0	0	0
η_3	.436	1.433	0	0	0	0
η_4	-.466	.194	-.111	0	0	.531
η_5	.416	.228	-.013	1.039	0	-.069
η_6	.630	.370	.179	1.367	-1.089	0

GAMMA (Structual Coefficients from Exogenous to Endogenous Variables)

	ξ_1
η_1	-.097
η_2	.446
η_3	-.563
η_4	.155
η_5	.071
η_6	.085

Table 19 (continued)

Squared Multiple Correlations (Reliabilities) of Indicator Variables and THETA's (Errors of Measurement)

	THETA EPS			THETA DELTA	
Variable	Rel.	Error	Variable	Rel.	Error
ELCHILD	.265	.735	GROUP	1.000	.000
CURREL	.736	.264			
YRSUS	.420	.580			
ELABL	.548	.452			
PAROCC	.305	.695			
PARED	.287	.713			
INCOME	.312	.688			
POSSESS	.398	.602			
PARSCHL	.230	.770			
PARPLAN	.714	.286			
VOCAB	.616	.384			
READING	.658	.342			
WRITING	.695	.305			
MATH	.697	.303			
SCIENCE	.671	.329			
CONCPT	.137	.863			
CONTRL	.273	.727			
MOT	.088	.912			

Squared Multiple Correlations of Structural Equations and Residuals

	SMC	Res.
η_1	.035	.256
η_2	.867	.041
η_3	.399	.138
η_4	.536	.286
η_5	.979	.015
η_6	.808	.026

Total Coefficient of Determination

For Y-variables	.997
For X-variable	——
For structural equations	.928

Measures of Goodness of Fit for the Whole Model

GFI index	.968
Adjusted GFI index	.953
Root mean square residual	.062

(.416). Lastly, being ethnic-language dominant did not seem to cause psychological alienation, as many advocates for cultural assimilation have claimed. In fact, preserving the ethnic language led to healthier orientation toward oneself as well as school (.630).

SES (η_2) turned out to be a facilitator of parental monitoring (1.433), psychological orientation (.370), quantitative learning (.228), and verbal learning (.194), in that order. That SES was a strong cause of parental involvement in the pooled-sample model contradicts with the results from the single-group analyses, suggesting a significant ethnicity effect, as was confirmed by the large GA(2,1) value to be discussed below.

Parental involvement (η_3), after partialing out ethnicity, did not affect either psychological orientation or academic achievement significantly. Its direct effects were all very small (from -.111 to -.179).

Verbal achievement (η_4) had a tremendous impact on quantitative learning for the language minority students (1.039). Proficiency in the English language was almost the determining factor of quantitative achievement. It also tended to promote positive psychological orientation (1.367) very strongly.

Perhaps the most baffling finding here is the negative effect of quantitative achievement (η_5) on psychological orientation (-1.089). Its effect was almost of the same magnitude as the effect of verbal achievement, but in the reverse direction.

Psychological orientation (η_6) affected verbal achievement positively (.531) but almost did not have any effect on quantitative achievement (-.069). This is in accord with the assertion that positive attitude toward the target language and culture determines success in the learning of the target language.

We now turn to the direct effects of group membership (ξ_1) on the six latent constructs in the gamma matrix. Being an Asian or Hispanic origin did not seem to make a difference in ethnic-language dominance (-.097), quantitative achievement (.071), or psychological orientation (.085). This means that the two groups did not differ much on ethnic-language dominance, quantitative achievement, and psychological orientation, although the Asian group tended to be a little less ethnic-language-dominant, somewhat more motivated, and performed a little better on quantitative achievement than the Hispanic.

Ethnicity, however, was a determining factor of socio-economic status (.446). Because the Asian group was coded as 1 and the Hispanic as 0, the positive value of GA(2,1) indicates that the Asian students tended to be socio-economically better off than the Hispanic. On the other hand, Asian parents tended to be much less involved in their children's academic study, as shown by the negative value of GA(3,1). Compared to the Hispanic students, the Asian students were slightly superior in their verbal achievement (.155).

Having interpreted the factor loadings and structural coefficients of the pooled-sample analysis, we now turn to the evaluation of the pooled-sample model. The reliabilities of the eighteen indicator variables varied from .088 for MOT to .734 for CURREL. These reliabilities can at best be considered minimally acceptable.

The squared multiple correlations of the six structural equations are all quite impressive, except for η_1 (.035), and probably η_3 (.399). This means that group membership explains almost none of the variance in ethnic-language dominance and less than 16% of the variance in parental involvement.

The other measures are all highly satisfactory: the total coefficient of determination for the Y variables was .997, for the structural equations was .928; the goodness of fit index was .968; the adjusted GFI was .953, and the root mean square residual was .062. (No chi-square statistics were reported because the ULS estimation method was used.) These all suggest that this model was a reasonably reliable and valid one.

The above parameter estimates of the pooled-sample covariance structure models are graphically presented in Figure 8.

It is worth reiterating that since pooling the two incompatible language minority groups was found to be empirically unjustifiable, the above results from the pooled-sample analysis should not be taken as contradictory to the previous findings from the single-group analysis. The large gamma estimates in the pooled-sample analysis and the large differences in the beta estimates between the single-group and pooled-sample analyses merely serve to provide further evidence that the Asian and

Figure 8. Parameter estimates of pooled-sample covariance structure model.

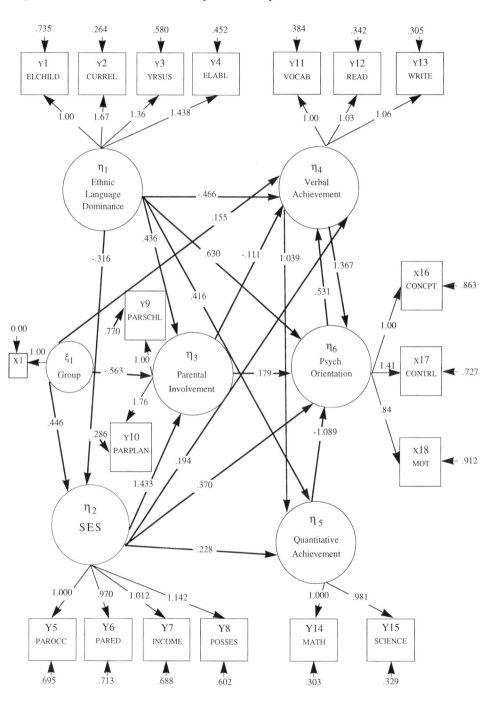

Hispanic students were very dissimilar in their achievement models. Generalization across ethnic groups should therefore be avoided when making claims about the causal relationships between the six latent constructs examined in this study.

Chapter Four

Discussion

This chapter is organized in exact correspondence to the previous chapter: first, the preliminary analysis, which includes the comparison between the random samples and their respective HSB populations, the exploratory factor analysis on the survey items measuring psychological orientation, and the simple statistics of the eighteen indicator variables; then, the confirmatory factor analysis by group, which provides the reliabilities of the indicator variables, and the reliabilities and validities of the final CFA models; next, single-group covariance structure analysis, which estimates the structural parameters of the final covariance structure models for each group; then, multi-group covariance structure analysis, which tests the invariance of the measurement models across the three ethnic groups; and lastly, pooled-sample covariance structure analysis, which assesses the effect of ethnicity on the six latent constructs in the covariance structure model with Asian and Hispanic students combined.

Preliminary Analysis

The results of the 35 univariate single-sample two-tailed z-tests in Table 5 clearly suggest that the random samples—one Anglo the other Hispanic—are representative of the respective HSB populations from which they were drawn. Although the Anglo sample was found to differ significantly ($p < .05$) from its population on Math Part I, and the Hispanic sample on Father Monitoring School, the ratio of significant differences (one out of 35 for each group) is so small that we can safely ignore these differences and conclude that the samples are representative of their populations.

Furthermore, we should also bear in mind that the N's in those significance tests are very large, ranging from 455 for the Anglo and 484 for the Hispanic to 16,231 for the Anglo and 2,150 for the Hispanic. Given the fact that the power of a significance test is a positive function of the sample size, in doing a large-sample significance test the alpha level should be set higher than usual, say, .01, to reflect the likelihood of rejecting a null hypothesis when in fact the difference is of minor practical significance. When such an alpha level is adopted, both of the above two significant differences become nonsignificant.

In light of the above discussion, none of those z-tests are meaningfully significant enough to warrant a rejection of the null hypothesis that the random samples represent their parent populations.

Because of the large number of variables involved, it would be a formidable task to perform a multivariate significance test of mean differences, even with the help of a sophisticated computing system. Judging from the large p-values of these univariate significance tests, we can safely infer that a multivariate significance test, although statistically more powerful, would have produced the same results—that the differences between the sample centroids and the population centroids are non-significant and therefore the random samples are representative of their parent populations.

In sum, the above discussion should provide us with enough evidence to claim that by analyzing the students randomly sampled from the HSB dataset, not much information was lost. In other words, any conclusion drawn from this study should be generalizable to the entire HSB populations. (However, see Chapter Five for some caution on the issue of generalizability.)

To empirically verify that the nineteen items on the survey which were presumed to measure psychological orientation were indeed reliable measures of three underlying factors—self-concept, internal locus of control, and motivation, a series of exploratory factor analyses were performed. For lack of significant factor loadings and consistency across groups, eleven of them were eliminated (see Table 6).

As a result of the small number of eligible items remaining, each of the three psychological factors is a composite of only two or three items. This partially explains why the reliabilities of the three psychological measures are so small (see Table 14). A direct consequence of the lack of reliability is that the parameter estimates in a covariance structure model become very unstable (Lomax, 1986). Had a larger set of items been used, the estimated structural parameters might have differed from what are reported in this study. This statement also holds true of the other latent constructs examined in this study.

An incidental finding of the exploratory factor analyses is that, upon closer examination, there is a tendency for the items phrased negatively to be measures of one common factor and the items phrased positively to be measures of another. For example, of the six items presumed to be measures of self-concept, items 1-4 are phrased positively; whereas items 5 and 6 are phrased negatively. It is no coincidence that items 1-4 tend to load on one factor and items 5-6 on another. The same can be said about the six items presumed to be measures of internal locus of control. Items 7-10 are negatively phrased whereas items 11-12 are positively phrased. Again, items 7-10 tend to load on one factor and items 11-12 on another.

The above finding should not come as a surprise to those who are familiar with the survey literature. It has been well documented that item phrasing plays a crucial role in determining the factor structure of the items under study (Benson & Hocevar, 1985). Therefore, instead of jumping to the conclusion that these items are not valid measures of their theoretical underlying factors, they should be studied more carefully to avoid the possible contamination of item phrasing effect.

Turning now to the simple statistics of the indicator variables, the simple means of the eighteen indicator variables presented in Table 9 provide interesting comparative profiles of the three ethnic groups. On ethnic-language dominance, Asian and Hispanic groups make equal use of English and their ethnic language during their childhood, but the Asian tend to be more vulnerable to mother tongue loss after they grow into their adolescent years. In addition, while the Hispanic have lived in the U.S. for a longer period of time than the Asian, they tend to rely more on their ethnic language for daily communication.

On socio-economic status, there seems to exist a trend of ethnic disparity. As frequently reported, Hispanic students typically come from socio-economically deprived families. Asian students' families, on the other hand, tend to be well-educated, enjoy prestigious occupations, and live in affluent conditions. On parental involvement, Asian parents are typically more involved in monitoring their children's academic study than are Hispanic and Anglo parents. This finding is consistent with the common observation that Asian parents tend to be very demanding about their children's performance in school.

On psychological orientation, Hispanic students tend to be less positively oriented toward themselves and schooling than are Asian and Anglo. This finding should not be surprising if we consider their relatively low SES and achievement. Asian students, on the other hand, typically take a more positive attitude toward themselves, despite their minority status. However, they do not feel as much in control of their environments as Anglos do—probably because their parents practically run their lives for them.

On cognitive achievement, Asian students do not appear to be jeopardized by their language minority status. Anglo students only have a slight edge over the Asian in reading, vocabulary, and science. When it comes to writing and math, Asian students even outperform their Anglo peers. Hispanic students, on the other hand, perform at a much lower level. On all five measures of cognitive achievement, the Hispanic not only fall behind their Asian and Anglo peers, but the differences are rather large—generally 4-6 times larger than the difference between the Asian and the Anglo.

A troublesome issue concerns the multivariate normal distribution assumption for covariance structure analysis. Even if the argument that multiple univariate normality tests reasonably approximate a single multivariate normality test, strong evidence is lacking that the significant D-statistics ($p < .01$ for 47 out of the 50 tests) represent non-serious violation to the assumption. Although the decision was to proceed with subsequent multivariate analyses without transformation, it must be borne in mind that the resulting ML estimates may not be reliable estimates and therefore chi-square statistics should not be used as the sole criterion in judging model fit.

We now turn to the correlations and generalized variances of the indicator variables. Because of the controversy over the role of ethnic language in minority education, special attention should be paid to the relationship between ethnic-language dominance and the other latent constructs. As seen in Table 10, measures of ethnic-language dominance are largely negatively correlated with measures of socio-economic status. This negative relationship can be further noted by the strong negative disattenuated correlations between the two underlying constructs reported in Table 17 (–.438 for the Hispanics and -.361 for the Asians). This finding confirms the observation that ethnic-language-dominant minorities tend to suffer from poorer socio-economic conditions.

Correlations between measures of ethnic-language dominance and parental involvement generally show a lack of interdependence. Single-group covariance structure analyses also indicate a small positive, but non-significant, effect of ethnic-language dominance.

Correlations between measures of ethnic-language dominance and psychological orientation are largely mixed. Perhaps one general trend is noteworthy: Language minority students tend to feel less in control of their environment when they have to rely on their ethnic language for communication, but they are no less motivated toward schooling, probably because they know they have to work hard to compensate for their language deficiencies. This tendency is somewhat stronger for the Asian than the Hispanic.

Correlations between measures of ethnic-language dominance and academic achievement are mostly negative. As would be expected, verbal performance appears to be more victimized by the use of ethnic language than does quantitative performance. An interesting finding is that when comparing the correlations between the two groups, we see a much weaker association between ethnic-language dominance and achievement for the Hispanic group than the Asian, suggesting that there may be other non-linguistic factors (such as SES) that account for more of the achievement variance for the Hispanic.

Turning to the generalized variances of the correlations used in the covariance structure analyses (Table 11), we can see that, although none of them are too small for ML estimation to apply, they are nevertheless fairly close to zero, especially for the Asian group. This suggests that multicollinearity may exist in the covariance structure models, resulting in large standard errors (see Table 17). It is no coincidence that the standard errors of the parameter estimates are particularly high for the Asian group.

Multicollinearity represents a classical example of threat to substantive interpretation in multivariate causal analysis. Most of the findings in this study, then, should be regarded as suggestive rather than conclusive.

Confirmatory Factor Analysis

The results of the confirmatory factor analyses suggest that simple models with no complex loadings do not hold well (see Table 12). For the exogenous variables, parental education loads not only on socio-economic status but also ethnic-language dominance. For the endogenous variables, internal locus of control loads on parental involvement in addition to psychological orientation. These complex loadings, however, are not consistent across groups. Parental education is a complex variable only for the Asian group, and internal locus of control is only marginally complex for the Anglo.

The specification search in the confirmatory factor analyses of the exogenous and endogenous variables has yielded quite reasonable fit. For the final modified models, all the chi-square values are brought under the significance level of .001. The unadjusted GFI values are all above .90, and the adjusted GFI values above .83. The root-mean-square residuals are all well controlled under .08. The χ^2/df ratios are kept under 2.5. All these indices suggest that the modification procedures have yielded quite satisfactory final CFA models.

There is, however, some uncertainty about the issue of correlated measurement errors. Throughout the searching process, no measurement errors were allowed to correlate, despite their high modification indices (see Table 13). Whether this zero-correlation constraint should be relaxed remains an unresolved question.

As an after-thought, perhaps allowing some of the measurement errors to correlate is not totally ungrounded. For example, since self-reported ethnic-language ability (ELABL) and current ethnic-language ability (CURREL) were obtained from each respondent at the same time, by the same instrument, and both measuring the "current" status, they probably shared the same response bias (Wardrop, personal communication, February 1988). Therefore, the possibility of relaxing the parameter estimate of the correlated measurement error between ELABL and CURREL probably should have been explored.

Turning to the reliabilities of the indicator variables in the final models, we see large variability among them (see Table 14). Academic achievement measures were on the whole very reliably measured by the five cognitive tests. The least reliable measures relate to psychological orientation, particularly self-concept and motivation. This raises the question of whether the exploratory factor analysis has failed in its attempt at helping form more reliable measures of psychological orientation.

Another concern relates to the "Heywood case," or negative error variance estimates. Improper solutions can arise from sampling variability, inaccurate data, unsubstantiated theory, or inappropriate form of analysis (Dillon & Goldstein, 1984, p. 488). That greater-than-one squared multiple correlations were produced for the endogenous variables may suggest that the simple-factor-structure model simply does not hold, resulting in serious model-data misfit.

Lastly, we return to Table 15 for the reliabilities and validities of the measurement models. The model reliabilities are all very high, indicating a strong joint relationship in each model. The model validities, however, are not as impressive, with the majority of them falling in the range of .452 to .577. It has been suggested that if the validity is less than .50, the validity of the measurement model is suspect since it means that the variance due to measurement error is larger than the variance captured by the construct(s) (Johnson & Wichern, 1982, p. 480). Therefore the measurement models for the exogenous variables might be less than valid, particularly so for the Hispanic group since more than 70% ($1 - .298 = .702$) of the average variance is due to error.

Single-Group Covariance Structure Analysis

As has been discussed extensively in Chapter Two, the initial single-group covariance structure models are underidentifed. Given that no instrumental variables in the HSB data set could be located, there were very few options left to battle the underidentification problem. The strategy adopted in this study was to use the parameter estimates of the underidentifed model as reference and fix one of the reciprocal paths to the estimated value. By so doing, simultaneous estimation was avoided and the model became identified.

This strategy, however, is not without concern. Although identified parameter estimates have been shown to be invariant over model identification, underidentifed parameter estimates are given "somewhat arbitrary values" (Jöreskog & Sörbom, 1984, p. III.77). The extent of such "arbitrariness," however, is not known. This means that the underidentified parameter estimates may or may not be reliable estimates. In other words, we have no assurance that, say, BE(4,3) of the Asian group, indeed has a true value of close to .353, since BE(4,3) is an unidentified parameter in the initial model (see Table 16).

What is also unknown is the extent of the effect of an unreliable parameter estimate on the other parameter estimates in the model. What would happen to the other parameter estimates if, say, the true parameter of BE(4,3) for the Asian group was really .250 instead of .353? To explore this issue, several values ranging from .250 to .450 were fed into the program as the BE(4,3) parameter. Fortunately, the resulting parameter estimates remained fairly stable. Therefore, as long as the arbitrariness of the unidentified parameter estimates generated by LISREL is within a reasonable range, the strategy used in this study to make an underidentifed model identified seems justifiable.

Another concern relates to the structural coefficients greater than 1 (see Table 17). When the correlation matrix is used as the input matrix for the LISREL analysis, all parameter estimates are "standardized" coefficients, which most commonly fall in the range of −1 to +1.

What, then, could explain those standardized structural coefficients being greater than one? Since structural coefficients in a causal model can be calculated and interpreted in exactly the same way as the regression coefficients in a regression model, I will use an example from regression analysis to illustrate the case. The standardized regression coefficient of X_1 in a multiple regression equation predicting Y from X_1 and X_2 can be computed as follows:

$$b^* = \frac{r_{y1} - r_{y2}\, r_{12}}{1 - r_{12}^2}$$

When r_{y1} and r_{12} are large and r_{y2} is small, b^* can be greater than one. For example, let $r_{y1} = .9$, $r_{12} = .6$, and $r_{y2} = .3$, then $b^* = 1.125$. The general rule is that when $r_{y2} < (r_{12}^2 + r_{1y} - 1) / r_{12}$, then $b^* > 1$ (Tatsuoka, personal communication, December 1987). Therefore some unique pattern of the correlation matrix of the latent variables *can* result in greater-than-one standardized structural coefficients.

Although it has been demonstrated above that theoretically standardized structural coefficients can take on greater-than-one values, such values still present a threat to interpretation. As can be seen in Table 17, greater-than-one structural coefficients are typically associated with large standard errors. In some extreme cases, the standard errors are even greater than the parameter estimates themselves, e.g., BE(2,4) and BE(3,4) in the Asian model. These large standard errors mean that the parameter estimates are highly unstable. They serve to caution us that care must be exercised in interpreting the parameter estimates. Non-significant parameters, if associated with large standard errors, should not be taken to mean non-significant effects; they simply suggest that the parameter estimates are not reliable.

One question remains: Why did those greater-than-one structural coefficients and large standard errors occur? They are
indicative of a phenomenon that commonly plagues multivariate research—"multicollinearity." It can be recalled that the
generalized variances of the correlations reported in Table 11
are all very small for the exogenous and endogenous variables
combined (.00021 for the Asian, .00683 for the Hispanic, and
.00887 for the Anglo), suggesting the possibility of "multicollinearity" in the antecedent variables (Pedhazur, 1982).
Unfortunately, little is known about how to deal with the multicollinearity problem.

Another precaution is in order: The standardized coefficients, although being scale-free and therefore comparable
across variables, are population-specific and therefore cannot
be used for comparison across groups (Duncan, 1975). Accordingly, the standardized solutions reported in Table 17 should be
used only for comparing the effects of different variables within
the same causal model. Whenever group comparison is suggested, it should be based on the relative ordering of effects
within each group rather than across.

With the above cautions in mind, we now turn to the substantive interpretations of the parameter estimates in the single-
group covariance structure models.

Factor loadings of the endogenous variables suggest that all
ten observed endogenous variables are significant measures of
their respective underlying factors. The only exception is the
complex loading of CONTRL on η_1, i.e., LY(9,1), which
although large in magnitude, has a large standard error. Its
large negative value suggests that internal locus of control loads
negatively on parental involvement. This holds true, however,
only for Hispanic and Anglo students. Asian students, interestingly enough, do not feel less in control as a result of parental
involvement, probably because of their unique cultural tradition
of obedience to authority.

Factor loadings of the exogenous variables also indicate that
all eight observed exogenous variables are significant measures
of their respective underlying factors. The complex loading of
PARED on ξ_1, i.e., LX(6,1), suggests that high level of parental
education reflects heavy use of the ethnic language. This holds

true only for Asian students, probably because most Asian-origin parents are first-generation immigrants who have received higher education in the U.S., but still retain their strong bond to the ethnic language.

We now turn to the central focus of the study—the causal linkages among ethnic-language dominance, SES, parental involvement, psychological orientation, verbal and quantitative achievements. The discussion that follows goes beyond direct effects to cover indirect effects also. This was judged necessary because causal analysis is very much "context-dependent" in that the direct effect of one factor on another tends to vary substantially depending on the other factors in the causal model. Therefore no discussion on the effect of a causal factor would be complete without examining the total effect (i.e., direct plus indirect effects). Decomposition of the total effects in the single-group covariance structure analysis is given in Table 20.

In accord with the intuitive appeal, ethnic-language dominance does hinder directly the learning of a second language (in this case, English) to some degree. It has been widely documented that interference from the native language should be held accountable for the learning difficulties of many language minority students in the U.S. (cf., Iglesia, 1985; Jensen, 1962; Laosa, 1984; Shepard *et al.*, 1983). Such direct negative influence from the ethnic language appears to strike Asian students to a greater extent than Hispanic students. This should not be surprising since, after all, Spanish is one of the Indo-European languages with many cognates of English words.

What advocates of bilingual schooling have observed in the positive effect of ethnic language on the English language performance, then, is only attributable to the indirect effect of ethnic language through psychological orientation. Studies that have shown positive relationship between proficiencies in the ethnic language and the English language (cf., Collier, 1987; Cummins, 1982; Ramirez & Politzer, 1976; Swedo, 1987) fail to make the important distinction between direct and indirect effects. The data in this study show that it is only through the positive effect on psychological orientation that ethnic language can function as a facilitator of second-language learning. O'Grady (1987), for example, acknowledged the value of the

Table 20
Decomposition of Total Effects in Single-Group Covariance Structure Analysis

	Group		
	Asian	Hispanic	Anglo
Ethnic-language dominance on verbal achievement			
Direct	−.258	−.160	
Indirect	.111	.047	
Total	−.147	−.113	
Ethnic-language dominance on quantitative achievement			
Direct	−.080	.166	
Indirect	.066	−.234	
Total	−.014	−.068	
SES on verbal achievement			
Direct	−.060	.150	.632
Indirect	.067	−.042	−1.399
Total	.007	.108	−.767
SES on quantitative achievement			
Direct	−.040	.099	.619
Indirect	.154	−.116	.123
Total	.114	−.017	.742
Parental involvement on verbal achievement			
Direct	−.412	−.751	−2.422
Indirect	.472	.696	2.187
Total	.060	−.055	.235
Parental involvement on quantitative achievement			
Direct	−.502	.120	−2.205
Indirect	.509	−.861	2.209
Total	.007	−.741	.004
Psychological orientation on verbal achievement			
Direct	2.462	1.564	3.384
Indirect	0	0	0
Total	2.462	1.564	3.384
Psychological orientation on quantitative achievement			
Direct	2.289	−.223	3.425
Indirect	-.254	1.587	0
Total	2.035	1.364	3.425

mother tongue from a psychological perspective, stating that the use of the ethnic language enhances second-language learning because it lessens anxiety and restores self-esteem. However, such indirect positive effect through psychological orientation tends to be too weak to offset the direct negative effects of ethnic language on learning the English language.

Ethnic-language dominance, on the other hand, has a direct positive effect on quantitative achievement for the Hispanic but a negligible negative effect for the Asian. This provides partial support to the assertion that, at least as far as Hispanic students are concerned, linguistic and cognitive development in the ethnic language helps promote quantitative learning, once we partial out the intervening effect of English proficiency.

However, when the indirect effects of ethnic-language dominance on quantitative achievement are taken into account, the small positive effect vanishes. Primarily through the strong impact of English proficiency on quantitative learning, ethnic language indirectly hinders quantitative achievement, leaving the total effect negligible.

This finding of negligible total effect of ethnic language on quantitative achievement provides disconfirming evidence to Cummins (1982) and others' (e.g., Chesarek, 1981; Yee & La Forge, 1974) strong claim that ethnic-language development promotes not only literary skills in both languages but also cognitive development in general. No such effect was found in this study. This suggests that a rigorous analytical methodology such as the causal modeling technique employed in this study may provide more accountable evidence for making causal inference than simple frequency or correlational analysis.

The effect of English achievement on quantitative achievement differs tremendously among the three ethnic groups. For Hispanic students, poor English proficiency jeopardizes quantitative learning in that language to a substantial extent. This strong causal relation between verbal and quantitative learning in the English language prompts educators of limited-English-proficiency students to place strong curricular emphasis on enhancing their English skills. For Asian students, their achievement in quantitative subjects depends to a much less extent on their English proficiency. In fact, verbal-oriented

Asian students tend to be slower learners in quantitative subject matters. For Anglo students, the causal relationship between verbal and quantitative learning is much less clear, due to the difficulties involved in the process of estimating underidentifed parameters.

It should be noted that the above findings do not necessarily provide disconfirmation to studies that have found positive effects of exposure to parallel language systems on general cognitive development of speakers of the majority language learning a foreign language, for example, English-speaking American students learning Spanish in a U.S. high school (Lambert, 1978; Rafferty, 1986). Such a context is likely to be an "additive" bilingual environment, as contrasted with a "substractive" bilingual environment for language minority students learning the majority language (Lambert, 1977). Therefore, interpretation of the present finding must be carefully confined to the intended target population of this study—language minority students in the U.S. high school system.

The effect of SES on achievement also varies to a great extent among groups. For Asian students, SES does not determine directly how they do in school. However, SES does exert a small positive indirect effect on achievement mediated by parental involvement and psychological orientation. Therefore, the total effect of SES on achievement for Asian students is small and positive. For Hispanic students, SES has a small positive direct effect on achievement. Its indirect effects through parental involvement and psychological orientation cancel each other out, leaving the total effect almost negligible. For Anglo students, SES is a direct positive contributing factor to school success or failure. However, because of the powerful negative effects on verbal achievement mediated by parental involvement, the total effect of SES on verbal achievement is strongly negative. The total effect of SES on quantitative achievement remains the same as its direct effect.

This finding, generally in agreement with some earlier studies on the differential effects of SES on educational outcomes of different ethnic groups, suggests that when studying the effect of SES on school learning, care must be exercised in drawing generalized conclusions across ethnic group. Studies that have documented a strong effect of SES should be recast in careful consideration of racial differences. Care also must be exercised in differentiating direct effect from indirect effect.

Contrary to the popular notion that parental involvement plays a positive role in effecting improved learning, the data examined in this study indicate a strong undesirable direct effect of parental involvement on school achievement. In fact, there is a direct tendency for students with demanding parents to perform less satisfactorily in school. However, parental involvement does foster positive psychological orientation, and through this path, indirectly bring about improved learning.

In most cases, the direct negative effect of parental involvement on achievement is offset by the indirect positive effect through psychological orientation, resulting in negligible total effect. The only exception is the effect of parental involvement on quantitative learning for the Hispanic, for whom the direct effect is small positive whereas the indirect effect is strongly negative, leaving a substantial negative total effect.

The above finding serves to cast a cautionary look at the studies that make the strong claim that parental involvement benefits student achievement (Epstein, 1986; Hewison & Tizard, 1980). Henderson (1987), in particular, reports that parental involvement in almost any form has a beneficial impact on students' achievement. This study shows that the benefits of parental involvement accrue only if it promotes positive orientation toward schooling and psychological being. It is therefore important to acknowledge that parental participation in school study and program planning must be carried out in such a way that positive attitude and motivation can be fostered (U.S. Department of Education, 1987).

It should be noted, however, that this direct negative effect of parental involvement on school learning should not be taken as an unambiguous evidence against studies that have advocated increased degree of parental involvement in their children's learning (e.g., Crespo & Lougue, 1984; Stearns, Peterson, Robinson, & Rosenfeld, 1973). For one thing, these studies typically operationalized parental involvement as parents participating in extracurricular activities, volunteering fund-raising services, and observing classroom activities. Had this study operationalized parental involvement accordingly, a positive effect might have emerged. For another, recall that in the causal models examined in this study, the relationship between parental involvement and academic achievement was hypothesized to be unidirectional, with parental involvement affecting achievement. One would be well justified to speculate that the other direction may also exist, with school achievement affecting parental involvement. If parents intervene only after problems occur, it should not be surprising that their intervention may be perceived negatively by their children and result in no miraculous solution for the learning problems.

On the issue of the causal relationship between psychological orientation and academic achievement, this study has found some interesting results. The causal link between the two appears to be uni-directional rather than bi-directional. There is no evidence that achievement affects psychological orientation to any extent, except for perhaps a very small positive effect on quantitative achievement for Asian and Anglo students. In other words, there is no support in this study for the causal precedence of academic achievement over psychological orientation, as several studies have claimed (cf., Burstall *et al.*, 1974; Savignon, 1972; Scheirer & Kraut, 1979; Strong, 1984). It is interesting to note that the level of proficiency in the majority language (English) does not seem to have any effect on the psychological well-being of the language minority student.

Positive attitude and high motivation, on the other hand, do bring about success in both verbal and quantitative learning, and the effect is quite substantial. The only exception is the small but negative direct effect of psychological orientation on quantitative achievement for Hispanic students. However, when the indirect effect mediated by verbal achievement is taken into consideration, the total effect becomes strongly positive.

The above finding of uni-directional causality between psychological orientation and school achievement provides strong support to the studies that have demonstrated causal precedence of psychological orientation over achievement; i.e., academic success is an outcome of positive psychological orientation rather than a necessary mediating factor for positive orientation to occur (Anderson & Evans, 1974; Dweck, 1975; Gardner, 1979; Krashen, 1982; Lambert, 1967; Song & Hattie, 1984).

It should be borne in mind that the above findings are based on a causal model in which the two exogenous factors (ethnic-language dominance and SES, in the case of language minority students) are assumed to be correlated. Since the correlations between the two factors are quite strong (−.361 for the Asian and −.438 for the Hispanic), there could be spurious effects in addition to the direct and indirect effects discussed above. This issue will be discussed more fully in the section dealing with the pooled-sample analysis.

Multi-Group Covariance Structure Analysis

Multi-group covariance structure analysis was used in this study to test the invariance between groups. Evidence for group differences has been seen in the specification search process in the exploratory factor analysis (see Table 12). That freeing a factor loading significantly improved the fit for one group but not another already provides some initial evidence that the parameters are not invariant across the three ethnic groups. This is further confirmed by the multi-group covariance structure analysis presented in Table 18. The three groups differ significantly in their measurement models, which precludes the possibility and need to test the invariance of their structural equation models. Thus, the third hypothesis that the three ethnic groups are not invariant (see Chapter One) is upheld.

Hispanic and Asian groups, in particular, seem to be very dissimilar—they failed even the least stringent hypothesis test of invariance of factor loadings. Interestingly, the two language minority groups resemble the language majority group to a greater extent than they resemble each other. This contradicts the assumption that, from the perspective of both being language minorities, Asian and Hispanic groups should resemble each other more than either group resembles the Anglo.

More specifically, Asian and Anglo students seem to have similar factor loadings for both the exogenous and endogenous variables, but their measurement errors differ significantly.

Hispanic and Anglo students have dissimilar factor loadings for the exogenous variables, but they resemble each other not only in their factor loadings but also their measurement errors of the endogenous variables.

The above finding does not uphold the fourth hypothesis that Asian and Anglo students are more similar to each other than are Hispanic and Anglo (see Chapter One). Despite the more comparable socio-economic and academic status between Asian and Anglo students, the two groups turned out to be very dissimilar in the interaction patterns of the latent constructs at work.

However, this finding of the two language minority groups being more similar to the language majority group than to each other needs to be examined more carefully. It must be remembered that different model specifications were employed in the multi-group analysis. In comparing the two language minority groups, six latent constructs and eighteen indicator variables were involved; whereas in comparing one of the language minority groups with the language majority group, only five latent constructs and fourteen indicator variables were involved. As has been discussed in the Methodological Review section in Chapter One, when evaluating competing structural models, the number of constructs in each of the models being compared should be the same; otherwise the model with fewer constructs is always likely to fit the data better because of the reduction in degrees of freedom. With this in mind, it should not be surprising to find that the multi-group model for the minority/ majority comparison fits the data better than the multi-group model for the minority/minority comparison (Harnisch, personal communication, February 1988).

Nevertheless, the findings from the multi-group analysis still argue for separate treatment of different minority groups. In other words, a generic model of academic achievement across ethnic groups is not likely to exist. Before further evidence can be found to argue otherwise, any claims about the effects of some hypothesized causal factors should be confined to a single group only.

We shall now turn to the discussion on the pooled-sample covariance structure analysis in which the ethnicity effect is further examined.

Pooled-Sample Covariance Structure Analysis

There are two advantages of incorporating ethnicity into the causal model: (a) By examining the magnitude and direction of the coefficients going from ethnicity to the other latent constructs, we can determine how the groups compare with each other; (b) by examining the magnitude and directions of the coefficients among the six latent constructs, we can determine the net effects of the latent constructs on each other after partialling out ethnicity.

The results of the pooled-sample analysis for the Asian and Hispanic groups combined are somewhat surprising (see Table 19). For example, while there may be little theoretical ground to speculate that Asian and Hispanic students differ in their ethnic-language dominance and psychological orientation, it is quite unexpected to find that they do not differ in quantitative achievement. This contradicts with many studies which have compared the school performance of different ethnic groups and found a superior performance of the Asian group. This study has found only a very slightly superior performance in quantitative achievement for the Asian group.

One possible explanation for this finding of comparable performance between Asian and Hispanic could lie in sampling bias. It should be recalled that a large number of students in the HSB dataset were excluded from this study for incomplete data. It is reasonable to speculate that those remaining in the study may share common characteristics—including similar academic performance.

On the other latent constructs, that Asian students have a definite advantage over Hispanic students in their socio-economic background is hardly surprising. What is surprising is that Asian parents are a lot less involved in their children's academic life compared to the Hispanic. This again contradicts with the common belief that Asian parents tend to be highly involved in their children's educational progress.

This raises the question whether the construct of parental involvement adequately reflect what the term conveys. Perhaps the two items used for operationalizing parental involvement capture only a very narrow aspect of the construct—parental monitoring of school work and study program. This again reflects the constraints of operationalization a researcher must face when dealing with secondary data sources.

At any rate, the results of pooled-sample covariance structure analysis provides further evidence that ethnicity does play a crucial role in establishing a causal model of academic achievement. Group variability could partially explain why contradictory findings have been reported in the literature. It is therefore very important that generalization across ethnic groups be avoided when constructing or interpreting an achievement model.

Chapter Five

Conclusions and Recommendations

Conclusions

Due to the unique nature of this study, I will conclude with a summary of the major findings resulting from the interplay between substantive theory and methodological considerations. In light of the various procedural concerns raised in the causal modeling process, some recommendations for future research will be given at the conclusion of this chapter.

Substantive Conclusions

For language-minority students in the U.S. high school system, ethnic-language dominance has a definite and detrimental effect on verbal achievement in the majority language. Interference from the ethnic language appears to be a direct cause of the learning difficulties many language minority students—especially Asian origin—have experienced in the U.S. Maintenance of the mother tongue, on the other hand, promotes very small but positive orientation toward schooling and oneself, and through this mediating mechanism, facilitates English proficiency indirectly.

On the relationship between ethnic-language dominance and quantitative achievement, evidence is lacking that linguistic and cognitive development in the ethnic language helps promote quantitative learning in the majority language. The small positive direct effect of ethnic-language dominance on quantitative achievement for Hispanic students tends to be nullified by the intervening effect of English proficiency.

Therefore the benefits of maintaining the literary skills in the ethnic language accrue only if favorable psychological orientation can be fostered. However, the data in this study show that such indirect positive effect tends to be too small to compensate for the negative direct effect from ethnic-language dominance. This finding suggests that for language minority students in U.S. high school—Asian and Hispanic alike, the psycholinguistic context appears to be one of "substractive bilingualism". Acquisition and use of the majority language occurs in a manner that socially and psychologically limits possibilities for the linguistic and cognitive development of the individual (Duran, 1987).

The effect of SES varies substantially among ethnic groups. For Asian students, SES does not influence directly how they do in school; however, a small positive effect can be gained through parental involvement and psychological orientation. For Hispanic students, SES has a small but positive direct effect on achievement, but its indirect effects through the mediating factors cancel each other out, leaving only a negligible total effect. For Anglo students, SES is a direct positive contributing factor to school performance, which tends to be offset by the powerful negative effect mediated by parental involvement, resulting in a negative total effect.

A quite unexpected finding in this study is the strong undesirable direct effect of parental involvement on school achievement for all groups. Demanding parents tend to produce lower academic performance. However, parents actively involved in their children's school work do foster positive psychological orientation, and through this path, indirectly bring about improved learning. It is, therefore, important to acknowledge that parental participation in their children's school work and program planning must be carried out in a caring and thoughtful manner that is indicative of parent's genuine interest in their childrens' education and be mediated by the development of attitudes conducive to learning.

On the causal relationship between psychological orientation and academic achievement, this study has found a primarily unidirectional linkage between the two, with psychological orientation taking causal precedence over academic achievement. In other words, academic success is an outcome of positive psychological orientation rather than a necessary mediating factor for improved psychological orientation to occur. It is interesting to note that proficiency in the majority language does not seem to have any effect on the psychological well-being of language minority students. Superior quantitative achievement, on the other hand, has a small tendency to make Asian and Anglo students feel good about themselves and schools.

On the issue of comparability among different ethnic groups, preliminary analyses in the forms of means comparison, exploratory and confirmatory factor analysis already suggest that the three ethnic groups differ substantially in nature. Subsequent covariance structure analyses provide further evidence that ethnicity plays a significant role in causal studies of this kind. Racial differences, therefore, must be recognized in any attempt to establish a causal model of academic achievement.

Methodological Conclusions

Covariance structural analysis have provided several distinct advantages over conventional correlational analyses:

(1) By including multiple manifest variables for the latent constructs, the structural model approaches an elaborate, self-contained system. The unrealistic assumption of "infallible measurement" is avoided and the hierarchical ordering among the causal variables is maintained.

(2) Through rigorous testing of simultaneous causality, linear structural relations analysis can handle nonrecursive models and test the asymmetry of a correlated linkage. Direction of causality can thus be established from an observed variance-covariance matrix.

(3) By decomposing the total effect into direct and indirect effects, linear structural relations analysis enables us to differentiate a direct effect from an indirect effect. It is therefore possible to describe the effect of a causal factor in unambiguous terms.

(4) Through a hierarchical significance testing procedure, covariance structure analysis allows simultaneous parameter estimation of multi-group data. This not only provides efficient estimation of parameters, but also pinpoints where in the structural network the groups differ significantly.

Several methodological concerns have also been encountered in this study:

(1) Although efforts were made to construct a comprehensive causal model of academic achievement, no single system can

completely capture the complex phenomena at play. Failure to include all relevant causal factors of an effect in the model has been shown to result in biased structural estimates and erroneous causal inferences (James, 1980). Unfortunately, the degree to which the problem of unmeasured variables biases structural estimates is not known, rendering the functional relations probabilistic (Cook & Campbell, 1979).

(2) In this study cross-sectional data were used to draw causal inferences. Cross-sectional designs attempt to model causal processes that have already occurred via functional equations that employ fixed constants (Pindyck & Rubinfeld, 1976). Estimation of the fixed constants is justified only if the equilibrium-type condition (Namboodiri, Carter, & Blalock, 1975), or the stability of the structural model, has been established (Heise, 1975). Again, without further evidence we cannot argue that the structural model had reached a temporary state of constancy at the time of measurement.

(3) Operationalization of the indicator variables included in this study invites further scrutinization. As cautioned by Jacob (1984), differences between abstract concepts and concrete measures can be a major cause for misleading conclusions and erroneous misinterpretations. Primarily due to the secondary-analysis nature of this study, not all variables in this study were measured with theoretically sound operationalization in the HSB survey. Information on some of the constructs included in this study was not collected by the HSB survey. The detrimental effect of difficulties in operationalization is particularly evident in the low reliabilities of the measures of psychological orientation and parental involvement, due to, among others, the small number of items designed to measure these constructs. Unreliabilities of indicator variables have been shown to result in serious attenuation of parameter solutions and biased estimates (Blalock, Wells, & Carter, 1970; Lomax, 1986). Kenny (1979) suggested several conditions for the bias due to measurement error to be negligible: (a) the reliabilities are high, (b) the true causal effects are small, and (c) the intercorrelations between causal variables are low. None of them seems to be met by the data in this study. Had a different

operational procedure been adopted, a different set of parameter estimates may have been produced.

(4) An *a priori* check on the "order" and "rank" conditions for the structural equations had indicated that three out of the four structural equations involving simultaneous causality were underidentified. For lack of alternative solutions, the strategy adopted to combat this underidentification problem was to use the parameter estimates of the underidentified model as reference and fix one of the reciprocal paths to the estimated value. By so doing, simultaneous estimation was avoided and the model became identified. Since it has been shown that unidentified parameters are given "somewhat arbitrary values" (Jöreskog & Sörbom, 1984), the extent of such arbitrariness must be examined. After experimenting with several values adjacent to the produced estimate, it was concluded that the arbitrariness of underidentified parameter estimates generated by LISREL seems to be within a reasonable range.

(5) A definite threat to multivariate analysis is multicollinearity. High intercorrelations among causal variables result in a generalized variance of close to zero, large standard errors of estimate, and greater-than-one standardized structural coefficients. It has been shown that high multicollinearity may lead not only to serious distortions in the estimates of coefficients but also to reversals in their signs (Pedhazur, 1982). An obvious candidate to ameliorate the situation is to delete variables that have been identified as causes of high multicollinearity. However, deletion of variables from the model may lead to specification errors (Chatterjee & Price, 1977). As stated by Farrar and Glauber as early as 1967, no "instant orthogonalization" can be offered. Unfortunately, this statement probably still holds true today.

Recommendations

In view of the above methodological concerns, it would be highly desirable to duplicate this study with the following recommendations in mind:

(1) In the attempt to identify reliable measures of psychological orientation, the exploratory factor analysis needs to be

Figure 9. Possible multi-trait, multi-method model for psychological
          orientation items.

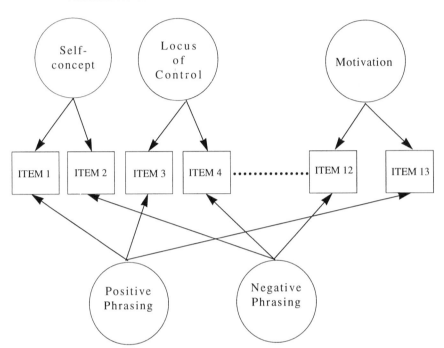

revised to take into account the possible item-phrasing effect.
A confirmatory factor analysis in the form of a multi-trait, multi-
method design as described in Zeller and Carmines (1980) and
practiced by Bachman and Palmer (1981, 1982) can provide a
much stronger and unambiguous argument for determining
the factor structure of the items. A possible model is described
in Figure 9.

(2) Special difficulty was encountered in the attempt to identify variables in the HSB Student File that measure parental
involvement. The only items used for operationalizing this construct are four items asking the student whether his or her
father and mother keeps close track of how well the student
does in school and how much the student talks to his or her
parents about planning school program. These items clearly
focus on only a very narrow aspect of the spectrum and may fail
to capture the conventional definition parental involvement

conveys. It is therefore highly recommended that other sources, such as the HSB Parent File, be explored to seek additional items to better represent the construct.

(3) In the process of specification for an optimal-fitting model, no errors of measurement were allowed to correlate, although the modification indices clearly suggested that freeing the theta parameters could yield significant fit improvement. This non-correlated-measurement-error constraint could be relaxed since the data were obtained from each respondent at the same time, by the same instrument, thus sharing the same source of response bias. Therefore, the possibility of relaxing some of the off-diagonal theta parameters should be explored and its effect on structural estimates should be examined.

(4) Lastly, the generalizability of the present findings should be further scrutinized. Recall that 50% of the eligible Asian students, almost 40% of the 600 randomly sampled Anglo students, and up to 60% of the 600 randomly sampled Hispanic students were deleted from the study for missing data on the 18 indicator variables. This raises the serious question of how comparable the students with complete data are to the students with incomplete data. For lack of evidence in this regard, the results from this study should be interpreted with the understanding that they may be unique to the subjects at hand and therefore may not be generalizable to the entire population. It is therefore highly recommended that this study be duplicated with a different set of subjects.

The above recommendations suggest fertile territory for future research on language minority achievement. Despite the methodological difficulties encountered in this study, the causal modeling technique holds great promise for examining a multivariate causal network in a more integrated manner than ever possible with any other conventional methodology. This study serves as a small step toward advancing our knowledge in the search for empiricism in education.

Notes

1 If the paths between psychological orientation and cognitive achievement had been hypothesized to be non-reciprocal, then either psychological orientation or cognitive achievement should have been treated as the only terminal outcome variable. Thus the parameter estimates would have been different from the model postulating reciprocal causality.

2 According to Willig, Harnisch, Hill and Maehr (1983), there are four kinds of causal attributions: ability, effort, luck, and task difficulty. These causal attributions correspond well to the common definitions of locus of control.

3 Since motivation was measured at the same time as final achievement, it would be more plausible to find a relationship between initial achievement and motivation but not motivation and final achievement.

4 Unfortunately, Gardner, Lalonde, and Pierson (1983) did not report the reliabilities of the achievement measures, although they did report the reliabilities of most of the other variables.

5 In reporting the significance level of the chi-square results, Parkerson, Lomax, Schiller, and Walberg (1984) indicated that the p value was less than .05. In actuality it was significant at a much higher level.

6 In factor analysis, standardized variance can be decomposed into:

1 = communality + specificity + measurement error.

In classical test theory, it can be represented as:

1 = reliability + unreliability,

where reliability = communality and unreliability = specificity + measurement error. Therefore, strictly speaking unreliability is not the same as measurement error. LISREL, however, does not distinguish the two and treat unreliability as measurement error.

7 What Dillon and Goldstein (1984) presented is a formula for computing the "average extracted variance" for a single construct. I took the liberty of extending it to multiple constructs to accommodate the possibility of a multiple-factor measurement model.

References

Anderson, J. G., & Evans, F. B. (1974). Causal models in educational research: Recursive models. *American educational research journal, 11*(1), 29-39.

Au, T. K. (1986). The effects of perceived parental expectations on Chinese children's mathematics performance. *Merrill-Palmer quarterly, 32*(4), 383-392.

Bachman, L. F. (1990). *Fundamental considerations in language testing.* Addison-Wesley.

Bachman, L. F., & Palmer, A. S. (1981). The construct validation of the FSI oral interview. *Language learning, 31,* 67-86.

Bachman, L. F., & Palmer, A. S. (1982). The construct validation of some components of communicative proficiency. *Teaching English to speakers of others languages (TESOL) quarterly, 16*(4), 449-465.

Backman, N. (1976). Two measures of affective factors as they relate to progress in adult second language learning. *Working papers on bilingualism,* No. 10.

Baral, D. P. (1979). Academic achievement of recent immigrants from Mexico. *National association of bilingual education (NABE) journal, 3,* 1-3.

Benson, J., & Hocevar, D. (1985). The impact of item phrasing on the validity of attitude scales for elementary school children. *Journal of Educational Measurement, 22*(3), 231-240.

Bentler, P. M., & Bonett, D. G. (1980). Significance tests and goodness of fit in the analysis of covariance structures. *Psychological bulletin, 88,* 588-606.

Bergan, J. R. (1980). The structural analysis of behavior: An alternative to the learning-hierarchy model. *Review of educational research, 50*(4), 625-646.

Bhatnager, J. (1980). Linguistic behavior and adjustment of immigrant children in French and English schools in Montreal. *International review of applied psychology, 29,* 141-159.

Biniaminov, I., & Glasman, N. S. (1983). School determinants of student achievement in secondary education. *American educational research journal, 20,* 251-268.

Blalock, H. M., Wells, C. S., & Carter, L. F. (1970). Statistical estimation with random measurement error. In E. F. Borgatta and G. W. Bohrnestedt (Eds.), *Sociological methodology.* San Francisco: Jossey-Bass.

Boomsma, A. (1982). The robustness of LISREL against small sample sizes in factor analysis models. In K. G. Jöreskog & H. Wold (Eds.), 1982.

Borgatta, E. F., & Bohrnestedt, G. W. (1970) (Eds.). *Sociological methodology.* San Francisco: Jossey-Bass.

Brickell, J. L. (1974). Nominated samples from public schools and statistical bias. *American educational research journal, 11*(4), 333-341.

Bridge, R. G., Judd, C. M., & Moock, P. R. (1979). *The determinants of educational outcomes: The impact of families, peers, teachers, and schools.* Cambridge, MA: Ballinger.

Burstall, C., Jamieson, M., Cohen, S., & Hargreaves, M. (1974). *Primary French in the balance: A report of the National Foundation for educational research in England and Wales.* Windsor, Berks: NFER Publishing.

Carroll, J. B. (1983). Psychometric theory and language testing. In J. W. Oller Jr. (Ed.), 1983.

Carter, T. P. (1970). *Mexican Americans in school: A history of educational neglect.* New Jersey: College Entrance Examination Board.

Castnell, L. A. (1983), Achievement motivation: An investigation of adolescents' achievement patterns. *American educational research journal, 20*(4), 503-510.

Chapman, J. W., & Boersma, F. J. (1979). Learning disabilities, locus of control, and mother attitudes. *Journal of educational psychology, 71,* 250-258.

Chatterjee, S., & Price, B. (1977). *Regression analysis by example.* New York: Wiley.

Cheng, L.-R. L. (1987). *Assessing Asian language performance: Guidelines for evaluating limited-English proficient students.* Rockville, MD: Aspen.

Chesarek, S. (1981). *Cognitive consequences of home or school education in a limited second language.* Paper presented at the Language Proficiency Assessment Symposium, Airlie House, VA.

Christian, C. C. (1976). Social and psychological implications of bilingual literacy. In A. Simoes (Ed.), *The bilingual child,* New York: Academic Press.

Clement, R. (1980). Ethnicity, contact, and communicative competence in second language. In H. Giles, W. P. Robinson & P. M. Smith (Eds.), *Language: Social psychological perspectives.* Oxford: Pergamon.

Collier, V. P. (1987). Students and second language acquisition. *NABE news,* 4-5.

Comber, L. C., & Keeves, J. (1973). *Science achievement in nineteen countries.* New York: Wiley.

Cook, T. D., & Campbell, D. T. (1979). *Quasi-experimentation: Design and analysis issues for field settings.* Chicago: Rand McNally.

Cooley, W. W. (1978). Explanatory observational studies. *Educational researcher, 7*(9), 9-15.

Crespo, O. Z., & Louque, P. (1984). *Parental involvement in the education of minority language children: A resource handbook.* Rosslyn, VA: InterAmerican Research Associates.

Cronbach, L. J., & Snow, R.E. (1977). *Aptitudes and instructional methods.* New York: Halstead Press.

Cummins, J. (1981). *Wanted: A theoretical framework for relating language proficiency to academic achievement among bilingual students.* Paper presented at Language Proficiency Assessment Symposium, Airlie House, VA.

Cummins, J. (1982). The role of primary language development in promoting educational success for language minority students. In California State Department of Education, *Schooling and language minority students: A theoretical framework* (pp. 3-50). Los Angeles: Evaluation, Dissemination, and Assessment Center.

Cummins, J. (1986). Empowering minority students: A framework for intervention. *Harvard educational review, 56*(1), 18-36.

Cummins, J., & Mulcahy, R. (1978). Orientation to language in Ukrainian-English bilingual children. *Child development, 4,* 1239-1242.

De Vries, J. (1985). Some methodological aspects of self-report questions on language and ethnicity. *Journal of multilingual and multicultural development, 6*(5), 347-368.

Dillon, W. R., & Goldstein, M. (1984). *Multivariate analysis: Methods and applications.* New York: John Wiley.

Drake, G. (1978). Ethnicity, values, and language policy in the United States. *NABE journal, 3*(1), 1-12.

Dulay, H. C., & Burt, M. K. (1978). *Why bilingual education? A summary of findings* (2nd ed.). San Francisco: Bloomsbury West.

Duncan, O. D. (1970). Partials, partitions, and paths. In E. F. Borgatta & G. W. Bohrnestedt (Eds.), 1970.

Duncan, O. D. (1975). *Introduction to structural equation models.* New York: Academic Press.

Duran, R. P. (1987). Factors affecting development of second language literacy. In S. R. Goldman & H. T. Hrueba (Eds.), *Becoming literate in English as a second language* (pp. 33-55). Norwood, NJ: Ablex.

Dweck, C. S. (1975). The role of expectations and attributions in the alleviation of learned helplessness. *Journal of personality and social psychology, 31*, 674-685.

Entwisle, D. R., & Baker, D. P. (1983). Gender and young children' expectations for performance in arithmetic. *Developmental psychology, 19*, 200-209.

Epstein, J. (1986). Parents' reaction to teacher practices of parent involvement. *The elementary school journal, 86*, 277-294.

Fiske, D. W. (1971). *Measures and concepts of personality.* Chicago: Aldine.

Flahive, P. E. (1980). Separating the g factor from reading comprehension. In J. W. Oller, Jr. (Ed.), *Research in language testing* (pp. 34-46). Rowley, MA: Newbury House.

Flores, S. H. (1978). *The nature and effectiveness of bilingual education programs for the Spanish-speaking child in the United States.* New York: Arno Press.

Foshay, W. R., & Misanchuk, E. R. (1981). Toward the multi-variate modeling of achievement, aptitude, and personality. *Journal of educational research, 74*, 353-357.

Fotheringham, J. B., & Creal, D. (1980). Family socioeconomic and educational-emotional characteristics as predictors of school achievement. *Journal of educational research, 73*(6), 311-317.

Fouly, K. A. (1985). *A multivariate study of the nature of language proficiency and its relationship to learner traits: A confirmatory approach.* Unpublished doctoral dissertation, University of Illinois at Urbana-Champaign.

Fuller, W. A., & Hidiroglou, M. A. (1978). Regression estimation after correcting for attenuation. *Journal of the American statistical association, 73*, 99-104.

Gallini, J. K. (1983). Misspecifications that can result in path analysis structures. *Applied psychological measurement, 7*(2), 125-137.

Gardner, R. C. (1979). Social psychological aspects of second language acquisition. In H. Giles & R. St. Clair (Eds.), *Language and social psychology.* Oxford: Basil Blackwell.

Gardner, R. C., Lalonde, R. N., & Pierson, R. (1983). The socio-educational model of second language acquisition: An investigation using LISREL causal modeling. *Journal of language and social psychology, 2*, 1-15.

Gardner, R. C., Lalonde, R. N., & MacPherson, J. (1985). Social factors in second language attrition. *Language learning, 35*(4), 519-540.

Genesee, F. (1978). Is there an optimal age for starting second language instruction? *McGill journal of education, 13*, 145-154.

Gnanadesikan, R. (1977). *Methods for statistical data analysis of multivariate observations.* New York: Wiley.

Grant, W. V., & Eiden, L. J. (1981). *Digest of education statistics, 1981.* Washington, DC: National Center for Education Statistics.

Griffin, L. J. (1977). Causal modeling of psychological success in work organizations. *Academy of management journal, 20,* 6-33.

Haertel, G. D., Walberg, H. J., & Weinstein, T. (1983). Psychological performance models of educational performance: A theoretical synthesis. *Review of educational research, 53,* 75-91.

Hansford, B. C., & Hattie, J. A. (1982). Relationship between self-concept and achievement/performance measures. *Review of educational research, 52,* 123-142.

Harman, H. H. (1976). *Modern factor analysis.* Chicago: University of Chicago Press.

Harmers, J. F., & Blanc, M. (1982). Toward a social-psychological model of bilingual development. *Journal of language and social psychology, 1*(1), 29-49.

Hartman, B. W., Eugua, D. R., & Jenkin, S. J. (1985-86). The problems of and remedies for nonresponse bias in educational surveys. *Journal of experimental education, 54*(2), 85-90.

Heckman, J. J., & McCurdy, T. E. (1984). *A simultaneous equations linear probability model.* Unpublished manuscript.

Heise, D. R. (1969). Problems in path analysis and causal inference. In E. F. Borgatta & G. W. Bohrnstedt (Eds.), *Sociological methodology 1969.* San Francisco: Jossey-Bass.

Heise, D. R. (1975). *Causal analysis.* New York: Wiley.

Henderson, A. (Ed.). (1987). *Parental participation–student achievement: The evidence grows.* Columbus, MD: National Committee for Citizens in Education.

Herman, G. (1980). Attitudes and success in children's learning English as a second language: The motivational vs. the resultative hypothesis. *English language teaching journal, 34*, 247-254.

Hewison, J., & Tizard, J. (1980). Parental involvement and reading attainment. *British journal of educational psychology, 50*, 209-215.

Heyns, B., & Hilton, T. L. (1982). The cognitive tests for High School and Beyond: An assessment. *Sociology of education, 55*, 89-102.

Husen, T. (1967). *International study of achievement in math: comparison of twelve countries.* New York: Wiley.

Iglesia, A. (1985). Communication in the home and classroom: Match or mismatch? *Topics in language disorders, 5*(4), 29-41.

IBM Corporation (1983). *CMS Primer, release 3* (2nd ed.). Endicott, NY: IBM Corporation.

Jacob, H. (1984). *Using published data: Errors and remedies.* Beverly Hills, CA: Sage.

James, L. R. (1980). The unmeasured variables problem in path analysis. *Journal of applied psychology, 65*, 415-421.

Jensen, J. V. (1962). Effects of childhood bilingualism, I. *Elementary English, 34*, 132-143.

Johnson, R. A., & Wichern, D. W. (1982). *Advanced multivariate statistical analysis.* Englewood Cliffs, NJ: Prentice-Hall.

Jöreskog, K. G. (1971). Simultaneous factor analysis in several populations. *Psychometrika, 36*, 409-426.

Jöreskog, K. G. (1978). Statistical analysis of covariance and correlation matrices. *Psychometrika, 43*, 443-477.

Jöreskog, K., & Lawley, D. N. (1968). New methods of maximum likelihood factor analysis. *British journal of mathematical and statistical psychology, 21*, 85-96.

Jöreskog, K. G., & Sörbom, D. (1984). *LISREL VI user's guide.* Chicago: Scientific Software.

Jöreskog, K. G., & Wold, H. (1982) (Eds.). *Systems under indirect observations: Causality, structure, and prediction.* Amsterdam: North Holland.

Kaiser, H. F. (1958). The varimax criterion for analytical rotation in factor analysis. *Psychometrika, 23*, 187-200.

Keith, T. Z., & Page, E. B. (1985). Do catholic high schools improve minority student achievement? *American educational research journal, 22*, 337-349.

Kenny, D. (1979). *Correlation and causality.* New York: Wiley.

Kitano, H. H. L. (1974). *Race relations.* Englewood Cliffs, NJ: Prentice-Hall.

Kmenta, J. (1971). *Elements of econometrics.* New York: Macmillian.

Krashen, S. D. (1982). Bilingual education and second language acquisition theory. In California State Department of Education, *Schooling and language minority students: A theoretical framework.* Sacramento, CA: Evaluation, Dissemination, and Evaluation Center.

Krashen, S. D., Long, M. A., & Scarcella, R. C. (1979). Age, rate, and eventual attainment in second language acquisition. *TESOL quarterly, 13*(4), 573-582.

Lambert, W. E. (1967). A social psychology of bilingualism. *Journal of social issues, 23*, 91-109.

Lambert, W. E. (1978). Some cognitive and sociocultural consequences of being bilingual. In J. E. Alatis (Ed.), *Interna-*

tional dimensions of bilingual education. Washington, DC: Georgetown University Press.

Lambert, W. E. (1977). The effects of bilingualism on the individual: Cognitive and sociocultural consequences. In P. A. Hornby (Ed.), *Bilingualism: Psychological, social, and educational implication* (pp. 189-224). New York: Academic.

Laosa, L. M. (1984). Ethnic, socioeconomic, and home language influences upon early performance or measures of abilities. *Journal of educational psychology.* *76*(6), 1178-1198.

Leamer, E. E. (1978). *Specification searches.* New York: Wiley.

Lohnes, P. R. (1979). Factorial modeling in support of causal inference. *American educational research journal, 16*(4), 323-340.

Lomax, R. G. (1982). A guide to LISREL-type structural equation modeling. *Behavior research methods and instrumentation, 14,* 1-8.

Lomax, R. G. (1983). A guide to multiple sample structural equation model. *Behavior research methods and instrumentation, 14,* 1-8.

Lomax, R. G. (1985). A structural model of public and private schools. *Journal of experimental education, 53*(4), 216-226.

Lomax, R. G. (1986). The effect of measurement error in structural equation modeling. *Journal of experimental education, 54*(3), 157-162.

Long, J. S. (1983a). *Confirmatory factor analysis.* Beverly Hills, CA: Sage.

Long, J. S. (1983b). *Covariance structure methods: An introduction to LISREL.* Beverly Hills, CA: Sage.

Lord, F. M., & Novick, M. R. (1968). *Statistical theories of mental test scores*. Reading, MA: Addison-Wesley.

Mace, B. J. (1972). *A linguistic profile of children entering Seattle public schools' kindergartens in September 1971 and implications for their instruction*. Unpublished master's thesis, University of Texas at Austin.

Mardia, K. V., Kent, J. T., & Bibby, J. M. (1979). *Multivariate analysis*. New York: Academic Press.

Marjoribanks, K. (1979). Ethclass, the achievement syndrome, and children's cognitive performance. *Journal of education research, 72*, 327-333.

Marjoribanks, K. (1985). Families, schools, and aspirations: Ethnic group differences. *Journal of experimental education, 53*(3), 141-147.

Mason, R., & Halter, A. N. (1971). The application of a system of simultaneous equations to an innovation diffusion model. In H. M. Blalock, Jr. (Ed.), *Causal models in the social sciences*. New York: Aldine.

Miller, D. C. (1970). *Handbook for research design and social measurement*. New York: David McKay.

Moore, E. G. J., & Smith, A. W. (1985). Mathematics aptitude: Effects of coursework, household language, and ethnic differences. *Urban education, 20*(3), 273-294.

Muthen, B. (1982). Some categorical response models with continuous latent variables. In K. G. Jöreskog and H. Wold (Eds.), 1982.

Muthen, B. (1982). Personal communication cited by Lomax (1985).

Namboodiri, N. K., Carter, L. R., & Blalock, H. M. (1975). *Applied multivariate analysis and experimental designs*. New York: McGraw-Hill.

National Center for Education Statistics (1984). *High School and Beyond, a national longitudinal study for the 1980's: Quality of responses of high school students to questionnaire items.* Washington, DC: National Center for Education Statistics.

National Opinion Research Center (1980). *High School and Beyond: Information for users, Base Year 1980* (Contract No. 300-78-0208). Chicago: National Opinion Research Center.

Nelson, F. H., Lomax, R. G., & Perlman, R. (1984). A structural equation model of second language acquisition for adult learners. *Journal of experimental education, 53,* 29-39.

Nielsen, F., & Fernandez, R. M. (1981). *Achievement and Hispanic students in American high schools* (contract No. 300-78-0208). Chicago: National Opinion Research Center.

Nielsen, H. D., Moos, R. H., & Lee, E. A. (1978). Response bias in follow-up studies of college students. *Research in higher education, 9,* 97-113.

Ogbu, J. U. (1978). *Minority education and caste.* New York: Academic Press.

O'Grady, C. (1987). Use of the learner's first language in adult migrant education. *Prospect, 2*(2), 171-181.

Oller, J. W., Jr. (1980). A language factor deeper than speech: More data and theory for bilingual assessment. In J. E. Alatis (Ed.), *Current issues in bilingual education* (pp. 14-30). Washington, DC: Georgetown University Press.

Oller, J. W., Jr. (1983) (Ed.). *Issues in language testing research.* Englewood Cliffs, NJ: Newbury House.

Oller, J. W., Jr., Perkins, K., & Murakami, M. (1980). Several types of learner variables in relation to ESL learning. In J. W. Oller, Jr. & J. Perkins (Eds.), *Research in language testing* (pp. 233-240). Rowley: Newbury House.

Olsson, U., & Bergman, L. R. (1977). A longitudinal factor model for studying change in ability structure. *Multivariate behavioral research, 12,* 221-241.

Page, E. B., & Grandon, G. M. (1979). Family configuration and mental ability: Two theories contrasted with U.S. data. *American education research journal, 16*(3), 257-272.

Parkerson, J., Lomax, R. G., Schiller, D. P., & Walberg, H. J. (1984). Exploring causal models of educational achievement. *Journal of educational psychology, 76*(4), 638-646.

Pascarella, E. T., & Chapman, D. W. (1983). A multiinstitutional, path analytic validation of Tinto's model of college withdrawal. *American educational research journal, 20*(1), 87-102.

Patkowski, M. (1980). The sensitive period for the acquisition of syntax in a second language. *Language learning, 30,* 449-472.

Patteson, B. J., & Wolfle, L. M. (1981). Specification bias in causal models with fallible indicators. *Multiple linear regression viewpoints, 11,* 75-89.

Pedhazur, E. J. (1982). *Multiple regression in behavioral research* (2nd Ed.). New York: Holt, Rinehart and Winston.

Peng, S. S., Owings, J. A., & Fetters, W. B. (1982). *Effective high schools: What are their attributes?* Washington, DC: U.S. Department of Education.

Pindyck, R. S., & Rubinfeld, D. L. (1976). *Econometric models and economic forecasts.* New York: McGraw-Hill.

Pottebaum, S. M., Keith, T. Z., & Ehly, S. W. (1986). Is there a causal relation between self-concept and academic achievement? *Journal of educational research, 79* (3), 140-144.

Purcell, E. T. (1983). Models of pronunciation accuracy. In J. W. Oller, Jr. (Ed.), 1983.

Rafferty, E. A. (1986). *Second language study and basic skills in Louisiana*. Baton Rouge, LA: Louisiana State Department of Education.

Ramirez, A. G., & Politzer, R. L. (1976). The acquisition of English and maintenance of Spanish in a bilingual education program. In J. E. Alatis & K. Twaddell (Eds.), *English as a second language in bilingual education*. Washington, DC: TESOL.

Rao, P., & Miller, R. C. (1971). *Applied econometrics*. Belmont, CA: Wadsworth.

Robinson, P. (1985). Language retention among Canadian Indians: A simultaneous equation model with dichotomous endogenous variables. *American sociological review*, *50*(4), 515-529.

Rosenthal, A. S., Meline, A., Ginsburg, A., & Baker, K. (1981). *A comparison of the effects of language background and socioeconomic status on achievement status among elementary school students* (contract No. 300-75-0332). Washington, DC: U.S. Department of Education.

Rumbarger, R. W. (1983). Dropping out of high school: The influence of race, sex, and family background. *American educational research journal*, *20*(2), 199-220.

Sang, F., Schmitz, B., Vollmer, H. J., Baumert, J., & Roeder, P. M. (1986). Models of second language competence: A structural equation approach. *Language testing*, *3*(1), 54-79.

SAS Institute (1987). *SAS applications guide* (1987 edition). Gary, NC: SAS Institute.

SAS Institute (1985a). *SAS user's guide: Basics* (1985 edition). Gary, NC: SAS Institute.

SAS Institute (1985b). *SAS user's guide: statistics* (1985 edition). Gary, NC: SAS Institute.

Savignon, S. (1972). *Communicative competence: an experiment in foreign language teaching.* Philadelphia: Center for Curriculum Development.

Scheirer, M. A., & Kraut, R. E. (1979). Increasing educational achievement via self-concept change. *Review of educational reseach, 49,* 131-150.

Schmitt, N. (1978). Path analysis of multitrait-multimethod matrices. *Applied psychological measurement, 2,* 157-173.

Schneider, S. G. (1976). *Revolution, reaction, or reform: The 1974 Bilingual Education Act.* New York: Las Americas.

Seginer, R. (1986). Mothers' behavior and sons' performance: An initial test of an academic path model. *Merrill-Palmer quarterly, 32*(2), 153-166.

Sellin, N. (1986). Partial least squares analysis. In J. P. Keeves (Ed.), Aspiration, motivation, and achievement: Different methods of analysis and different results. *International journal of educational research, 10,* 115-243.

Shavelson, R. J., & Bolus, R. (1982). Self-concept: The interplay of theory and methods. *Journal of educational psychology, 74,* 3-17.

Shepard, L. A., Smith, M. L., & Vojir, C. P. (1983). Characteristics of pupils identified as learning disabled. *American educational research journal, 20*(3), 309-333.

So, A. Y. (1983). The High School and Beyond data set: Its relevance for bilingual education research. *NABE journal, 7*(3), 13-21.

So, A. Y., & Chan, K. S. (1984). What matters? The relative impact of language background and socioeconomic status on reading achievement. *NABE journal, 8*(3), 27-41.

Song, I. S., & Hattie, J. (1984). Home environment, self-concept, and academic achievement: A causal modeling approach. *Journal of educational psychology, 76*(6), 1269-1281.

Sowell, T. (1978). Ethnicity in a changing America. *Daedalus,* 213-337.

Stearns, M. S., Peterson, S., Robinson, M., & Rosenfeld, A. (1973). *Parental involvement in compensatory educational programs: Definitions and findings.* Menlo Park, CA: SRI International.

Stephens, M. A. (1974). EDF statistics for goodness of fit and some comparisons. *Journal of the American statistical association, 69,* 730-737.

Stevenson, H. W., Stigler, J. W., Lee, S., Lucker, G. W., Kitamura, S., & Hsu, C. (1985). Cognitive performance and academic achievement of Japanese, Chinese, and American children. *Child development, 56,* 718-734.

Strong, M. (1984). Integrative motivation: A cause or result of successful language acquisition? *Language learning, 34,* 1-14.

Sue, S., & Zane, N. W. S. (1985). Academic achievement and socio-emotional adjustment among Chinese university students. *Journal of counseling psychology, 32*(4), 570-579.

Sue, D. W. (1973). Ethnic identity: The impact of two cultures on the psychological development of Asians in America. In S. Sue & N. Wagner (Eds.), *Asian-Americans: Psychological perspectives.* Ben Lomond, CA: Science and Behavior Books.

Swedo, J. (1987). Effective teaching strategies for handicapped limited English proficient students. *Bilingual special education newsletter, 6,* 2-5.

Thompson, W. W. (1985). Environmental effects on educational performance. *Alberta journal of educational research, 31*(1), 11-25.

Thurstone, L. L. (1947). *Multiple factor analysis.* Chicago, IL: University of Chicago Press.

Troike, R. (1978). Research evidence for the effectiveness of bilingual education. *NABE journal, 3*(1), 13-24.

Uguroglu, M. E., & Walberg, H. J. (1979). Motivation and achievement: A quantitative synthesis. *American educational research journal, 16*(4), 375-389.

U. S. Commission on Civil Rights (1975). *A better chance to learners: Bilingual bicultural education* (Clearinghouse publication No. 51). Washington, DC: Government Printing Office.

U. S. Department of Education, (1987). *Japanese education today.* Washington, DC: Government Printing Office.

Veltman, C. J. (1980). *Relative educational attainments of minority language children, 1976: a comparison to black and white English language children.* Washington, DC: National Center for Education Statistics.

Waggoner, D. (1981). Educational attainment of language minorities in the United States. *NABE journal, 6*(1), 41-53.

Walberg, H. J. (1978). *A psychological theory of educational productivity.* Invited paper read at the annual meeting of the American Psychological Association, Toronto.

Walberg, H. J., Hase, K., & Rasher, P. S. (1978). English acquisition as a diminishing function of experience rather than age. *TESOL quarterly, 12,* 427-437.

Walker, H. M., & Lev, J. (1952). *Statistical inference.* New York: Holt, Rinehart and Winston.

Wang, L. S. (1986). *Toward an explanatory model of minority achievement.* Master's equivalency paper, University of Illinois at Urbana-Champaign.

Wardrop, J. L., & O'Dell, L. L. (1985). *Structural equation modeling in educational research.* Unpublished manuscript. University of Illinois at Urbana-Champaign.

Wells, G. (1979). Describing children's linguistic development at home and at school. *British educational research journal, 5,* 75-89.

Wheaton, B., Muthen, B., Alwin, D. F., & Summers, G. F. (1977). Assessing reliability and stability in panel models. In *Sociological methodology* (ch. 3). San Francisco: Jossey-Bass.

Willig, A. C., Harnisch, D. L., Hill, K. T., & Maehr, M. L. (1983). Sociocultural and educational correlates of success-failure attributions and evaluation anxiety in the school setting for black, Hispanic, and Anglo children. *American educational research journal, 20*(3), 385-410.

Wold, H. (1982). Soft modeling: The basic design and some extensions. In K. G. Jöreskog, and H. Wold (Eds.), 1982.

Wolfle, L. M. (1980). Strategies of path analysis. *American educational research journal, 17*(3), 183-200.

Wolfle, L. M. (1981). *Causal models with unmeasured variables: An introduction to LISREL.* Paper presented at the annual meeting of American Educational Research Association, Los Angeles.

Wolfle, L. M. (1985). Postsecondary educational attainment among whites and blacks. *American educational research journal, 22*(4), 501-525.

Wolfle, L. M., & Robertshaw, D. (1983). Racial differences in measurement error in educational achievement model. *Journal of educational measurement, 20*(1), 39-49.

Wonnacott, R. J., & Wonnacott, T. H. (1979). *Econometrics.* New York: Wiley.

Wright, S. (1934). The method of path coefficients. *Annals of mathematical statistics, 5*, 161-215.

Yee, L. Y., & La Forge, R. (1974). Relationship between mental abilities, social class, and exposure to English in Chinese fourth graders. *Journal of educational psychology, 56*(6), 826-834.

Zeller, R. A., & Carmines, E. G. (1980). *Measurement in the social sciences*. Cambridge: Cambridge University Press.

Appendix A

HSB Base Year Data Files

School File

The School File contains school questionnaire responses that were provided by administrators in 988 public, Catholic, and other private schools. Each record has a total of 237 variables. The questionnaire focused on a number of school characteristics including type and organization, enrollment, faculty composition, instructional programs, course offerings, specialized programs, participation in federal programs, faculty characteristics, funding sources, discipline problems, teacher organizations, and grading systems.

Language File

The Language File contains information on each student who reported some non-English language experience either during childhood or at the time of the survey. This file contains 11,303 records and 42 variables for each student.

Parent File

The Parent File contains questionnaire responses from the parents of about 3,600 sophomores and 3,600 seniors who are on the Student File. Each record on the Parent File contains a total of 307 variables. Data on this file include parents' aspirations and plans for their children's postsecondary education.

Twin and Sibling File

The Twin and Sibling File contains responses from sampled twins and triplets; data on twins and triplets of sample members; and from siblings in the sample. This file contains 2,718 records and include all the variables in the HSB Student File.

Teacher Comments File

The Sophomore Teacher File contains responses from 14,103 teachers on 18,291 students from 616 schools. The Senior Teacher File contains responses from 13,683 teachers on 17,056 students from 611 schools. At each grade level, teachers had the opportunity to answer questions about sampled students who had been in their classes. The typical student in the sample was rated by an average of four different teachers. The file contains approximately 76,000 teacher observations of sophomores and about 67,000 observations of seniors.

Friends File
The Friends File contains identification numbers of students in the sample who were named as being friends. Each record contains the ID of sampled students and ID's of up to three friends. Linkages among friends can be used to investigate the sociometry of friendship structure, including reciprocity of choices among students in the sample, and for tracing friendship networks.

Appendix B

HSB Student Identification Pages

SO/SIP 4278
1980

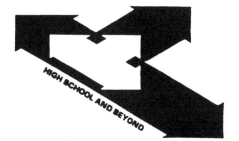

Form Approved
FEDAC No. S99
App. Exp: 12/80

High School and Beyond is sponsored by the National Center for Education Statistics, an agency of the United States Department of Education.

Thank you for accepting our invitation to participate in HIGH SCHOOL AND BEYOND. This is a voluntary but important national survey. We are pleased that you have agreed to participate. Your cooperation and participation will help us learn more about the experiences of high school students and their plans for the future.

All information which would permit identification of the individual will be held in strict confidence, will be used only by persons engaged in and for the purposes of this survey, and will not be disclosed or released to others for any purposes except as required by law.

STUDENT IDENTIFICATION PAGES

STATE:

SCHOOL NO:

STUDENT NO:

Prepared for the National
Center for Education
Statistics by the National
Opinion Research Center
NCE3 Form 2409-015

As a matter of policy, the National Center for Education Statistics is concerned with protecting the privacy of individuals who participate in voluntary surveys. We want to let you know that:

1. Section 406 of the General Education Provisions Act (20-USC 1221e-l) allows us to ask you the questions in this questionnaire.

2. You may skip any question you do not wish to answer.

3. We are asking you these questions in order to gather information about what happens to students as they move out of high school and make decisions about post-secondary education and work.

4. Your responses will be merged with those of other students, and the answers you give will never be identified as yours.

GENERAL INSTRUCTIONS

FOR QUESTIONS WHICH ASK YOU TO WRITE IN INFORMATION, PLEASE PRINT THE INFORMATION IN THE SPACE PROVIDED.

FOR OTHER QUESTIONS YOU ARE ASKED TO MARK A SQUARE. AN EXAMPLE IS:

What is your present high school class? (MARK ONE)

Freshman........................☐
Sophomore.....................■   If you are a Sophomore you would
Junior.............................☐   mark the square to the right of
Senior ....☐   Sophomore as shown.

1. Your name, address, and telephone number.

NAME:_____
　　　　　　　　Last　　　　　　　　　First　　　　　　Middle
ADDRESS:_____
　　　　　　　　Number　　　　　　　　Street

_____
　　　　　　　　Apt. No.

_____
　　　　　　　　City　　　　　　　　　State　　　　　Zip Code
TELEPHONE:_____
　　　　　　　　Area Code　　　　　　Telephone Number
(IF NO TELEPHONE. CHECK BOX ☐)

2. Your parent's or guardian's name, address and telephone number.
PARENT'S
(GUARDIAN'S) NAME_____
　　　　　　　　Last　　　　　　　　　First　　　　　　Middle
If address is same as yours, check box only and go to Q. 3. If different please fill in below.

ADDRESS:　　☐ Same as mine OR

_____
　　　　　　　　Number　　　　　　　　Street

_____
　　　　　　　　Apt. No.

_____
　　　　　　　　City　　　　　　　　　State　　　　　Zip Code
TELEPHONE:_____
　　　　　　　　Area Code　　　　　　Telephone Number
(IF NO TELEPHONE. CHECK BOX ☐)

3. Your date of birth: _____   _____   _____

                                      MONTH   DAY   YEAR

4. Your sex: (MARK ONE)   Male ....☐ 01
                                       Female ....☐ 02

5. Please write down the names of your three best friends in this school who are Sophomores. (Please use proper names, *not* nicknames.)

    WRITE FIRST AND LAST NAMES HERE.

    (1)_____

    (2)_____

    (3)_____

> The research staff would like to get in touch with you again to find out how your plans have worked out. To help us do so, we would appreciate your filling in the information on these next pages. This information will be kept in strict confidence and will only be used for future survey purposes.

6. Please print the name, address, and telephone number of a person (a relative, if possible) who lives at an address different from yours, who will always know where to get in touch with you.

    _____
    Name

    _____
    Number   Street

    _____
    City   State   Zip Code

    _____
    Area Code   Telephone Number

    Relationship to you:_____

7. Please print the name, address, and telephone number of another person who will always know where to get in touch with you (someone who lives at an address different from the one in question 6).

Name _____

Number _____ Street _____

City _____ State _____ Zip Code _____

Area Code _____ Telephone Number _____

Relationship to you:_____

8. Please print below your driver's license (automobile operator's or chauf-
    feur's license) identification number and the state in which it was issued.
    If you do not have a driver's license or don't know the number, please fill
    in one of the squares below.

                                        No driver's license...............☐ 01
    _____ _____ Don't know the number......☐ 02
    Identification Number   State Issued

9. Please print your Social Security number in the space below. If you do
    not have a Social Security number or don' know the number, plase fill in
    one of the squares below.

    > Giving us your Social Security number is completely volun-
    > tary, and there is no penalty for not disclosing it. It is
    > needed so that any later information gets correctly matched
    > with the same individual. We are authorized to ask these
    > questions by Section 406 of the General Education Provi-
    > sions Act (20 USC 1221e-1.

                                        No Social Security number..........☐ 01
    ☐☐☐ - ☐☐ - ☐☐☐☐   Do not know the number ....☐ 02
    Social Security Number   Do not wish to give the number..☐ 03

10. Do you have a nickname or some name other than your legal one by
    which most of your friends, neighbors or relatives know you? (MARK
    ONE)

        Yes ....☐ 01   (answer A)
        No ....☐ 02

        IF YES. What is it?   _____
                                      Nickname

The following questions are about the language or languages spoken by you
and your family.

11. What was the first language you spoke when you were a child? (MARK ONE)

English..☐ 01
Spanish...☐ 02
Italian...☐ 03
Chinese...☐ 04
French...☐ 05
German...☐ 06
Greek..☐ 07
Portuguese..☐ 08
Filipino languages..☐ 09
Polish...☐ 10

Other (Write in)_____☐ 11

12. What <u>other</u> language did you speak when you were a child — before you started school? (MARK ONE. IF MORE THAN ONE. MARK ONE MOST OFTEN SPOKEN.)

I spoke no other language...☐ 01

I also spoke:
English..☐ 02
Spanish...☐ 03
Italian...☐ 04
Chinese...☐ 05
French...☐ 06
German...☐ 07
Greek..☐ 08
Portuguese..☐ 09
Filipino languages..☐ 10
Polish...☐ 11

Other (Write in)_____☐ 12

13. What language do you <u>usually</u> speak <u>now</u>? (MARK ONE)
English..☐ 01
Spanish...☐ 02
Italian...☐ 03
Chinese...☐ 04
French...☐ 05
German...☐ 06
Greek..☐ 07
Portuguese..☐ 08
Filipino languages..☐ 09
Polish...☐ 10

Other (Write in)_____☐ 11

14. What language do the people in your home <u>usually</u> speak? (MARK ONE)
    English...☐ 01
    Spanish..☐ 02
    Italian..☐ 03
    Chinese..☐ 04
    French..☐ 05
    German..☐ 06
    Greek...☐ 07
    Portuguese ....☐ 08
    Filipino languages...☐ 09
    Polish ....☐ 10

    Other (Write in)_____☐ 11

15. What <u>other</u> language is spoken in your home? (MARK ONE. IF MORE THAN ONE <u>OTHER</u> LANGUAGE IS SPOKEN, MARK THE OTHER LANGUAGE WHICH IS SPOKEN MOST OFTEN.)

    No other langage is spoken ....☐ 01

    The other langage spoken is:
    English...☐ 02
    Spanish..☐ 03
    Italian..☐ 04
    Chinese..☐ 05
    French ....☐ 06
    German ....☐ 07
    Greek...☐ 08
    Portuguese ....☐ 09
    Filipino languages...☐ 10
    Polish ....☐ 11

    Other (Write in)_____☐ 12

16. Please look back at your answers to Questions 11 - 15 . . .

    . . . IF you answered ENGLISH (or no other language) to ALL FIVE QUESTIONS you have completed this section of the questionnaire. Thank you

    . . . If you answered a LANGUAGE OTHER THAN ENGLISH IN ANY OF THE FIVE QUESTIONS.* please write the name of <u>that language</u> here _____ then CONTINUE with the rest of this questionnaire. Most of the questions that follow are about the use of <u>that language</u> by you and your family.

* IF YOU ANSWERED MORE THAN ONE NON-ENGLISH LANGUAGE in Questions 11 - 15 please write the most important one on the line.

17. With regard to <u>that language</u>, how well do you do the following? (MARK ONE SQUARE FOR EACH LINE)

How well do you . . .	Very Well	Pretty Well	Not Very Well	Not at All
a. Understand <u>that language</u> when people speak it	☐	☐	☐	☐
b. Speak that language	☐	☐	☐	☐
c. Read that language	☐	☐	☐	☐
d. Write that language	☐	☐	☐	☐
	1	2	3	4

18. How often is <u>that language</u> spoken <u>by the peron underlined</u> in each of the situations listed below? (MARK ONE SQUARE FOR EACH LINE. IF YOU DO <u>NOT</u> LIVE WITH THE RELATIVE INDICATED OR DO NOT SEE THAT PERSON OFTEN, PLEASE MARK THE SQUARE UNDER "Does not apply.")

How often do (does):	Always or almost always	Mostly	About half the time	Some-times	Never	Does not apply
a. <u>You</u> speak that language to your mother	☐	☐	☐	☐	☐	☐
b. Your <u>mother</u> speak that language to you	☐	☐	☐	☐	☐	☐
c. <u>You</u> speak that language to your father	☐	☐	☐	☐	☐	☐
d. Your <u>father</u> speak that language to you	☐	☐	☐	☐	☐	☐
e. Your <u>parents</u> speak that language to each other	☐	☐	☐	☐	☐	☐
f. <u>Other relatives</u> (brothers, sisters, grandparents) speak that language around you	☐	☐	☐	☐	☐	☐
g. <u>You</u> speak that language with your best friends	☐	☐	☐	☐	☐	☐
h. <u>You</u> speak that language in school with other students	☐	☐	☐	☐	☐	☐

i. <u>You</u> speak that lan-
    guage in the stores
    you go to most of-
    ten (i.e., grocery rec-
    ord store, clothes
    store)........................☐...........☐.........☐..........☐...........☐...........☐......
j. <u>You</u> speak that lan-
    guage at work.........☐...........☐.........☐..........☐...........☐...........☐......
                        1   2   3   4   5   6

---

19. How well do you do the following? (ONE MARK SQUARE FOR EACH
    LINE)

	Very Well	Pretty Well	Not Very Well	Not at All
How well do you . . .				
a. Understand spoken English	☐	☐	☐	☐
b. Speak English	☐	☐	☐	☐
c. Read English	☐	☐	☐	☐
d. Write English	☐	☐	☐	☐
	1	2	3	4

EDUCATION IN THE UNITED STATES

This series of questions concerns subjects you may have had in school. Please
answer <u>only</u> for education you have received <u>in the United States</u>.

20. Did you have the following courses in <u>grades 1 - 6</u>? (MARK ONE
    SQUARE FOR EACH LINE)

	Yes	No	Not in the U.S. in grades 1-6
Did you have . . .			
a. An English course designed for students from non-English speaking backgrounds	☐	☐	☐
b. Reading and writing in <u>that</u> <u>language</u> (refer to Q. 16 for "that language")	☐	☐	☐
c. Other subjects, such as math or science, taught, at least in part, in <u>that language</u>	☐	☐	☐
d. Courses in the history and culture of your ancestors' country of origin or their life in the United States	☐	☐	☐
	1	2	3

21. Did you have the following courses in <u>grades 7 - 9</u>? (MARK ONE SQUARE FOR EACH LINE)

	Yes	No	Not in the U.S. in grades 7 - 9
Did you have . . .			
a. An English course designed for students from non-English speaking backgrounds	☐	☐	☐
b. Reading and writing in <u>that language</u> (refer to Q. 16 for "that language")	☐	☐	☐
c. Other subjects, such as math or science, taught, at least in part, in <u>that language</u>	☐	☐	☐
d. Courses in the history and culture of your ancestors' country of origin or their life in the United States	☐	☐	☐
	1	2	3

22. Did you have the following courses in <u>grades 10 - 12</u>? (MARK ONE SQUARE FOR EACH LINE)

	Yes	No
Did you have . . .		
a. An English course designed for students from non-English speaking backgrounds	☐	☐
b. Reading and writing in <u>that language</u> (refer to Q. 16 for "that language")	☐	☐
c. Other subjects, such as math or science, taught, at least in part, in <u>that language</u>	☐	☐
d. Courses in the history and culture of your ancestors' country of origin or their life in the United States	☐	☐
	1	2

23. Thinking about <u>all</u> the courses you had in each of those grades listed below, how much of the teaching was done in <u>that language</u>?

    A. <u>In grades 1 - 6</u>: (MARK ONE)

        All or almost all of the teaching

            was done in that language............................☐ 01

        Most was in that language...............................☐ 02

        About half was in that language ....☐ 03

        Some was in that language...............................☐ 04

        None was in that language..............................☐ 05

        Was not in school in U.S. then ....☐ 06

    A. <u>In grades 7 - 9</u>: (MARK ONE)

        All or almost all of the teaching

            was done in that language............................☐ 01

        Most was in that language...............................☐ 02

        About half was in that language ....☐ 03

        Some was in that language...............................☐ 04

        None was in that language..............................☐ 05

        Was not in school in U.S. then ....☐ 06

    C. <u>In grades 10 - 12</u>: (MARK ONE)

        All or almost all of the teaching

            was done in that language............................☐ 01

        Most was in that language...............................☐ 02

        About half was in that language ....☐ 03

        Some was in that language...............................☐ 04

        None was in that language..............................☐ 05

Appendix C

HSB Sophomore Questionnaire

SO/Q 4278
1980

Form Approved
FEDAC No. S99
App. Exp: 12/80

High School and Beyond is sponsored by the National Center for Education Statistics, an agency of the United States Department of Education.

Thank you for accepting our invitation to participate in HIGH SCHOOL AND BEYOND. This is a voluntary but important national survey. We are pleased that you have agreed to participate. Your cooperation and participation will help us learn more about the experiences of high school students and their plans for the future.

All information which would permit identification of the individual will be held in strict confidence, will be used only by persons engaged in and for the purposes of this survey, and will not be disclosed or released to others for any purposes except as required by law.

SOPHOMORE QUESTIONNAIRE

STATE:

SCHOOL NO:

STUDENT NO:

Prepared for the National
Center for Education
Statistics by the National
Opinion Research Center
NCE3 Form 2409-01

As a matter of policy, the National Center for Education Statistics is concerned with protecting the privacy of individuals who participate in voluntary surveys. We want to let you know that:

1. Section 406 of the General Education Provisions Act (20-USC 1221e-1) allows us to ask you the questions in this questionnaire.

2. You may skip any question you do not wish to answer.

3. We are asking you these questions in order to gather information about what happens to students as they move out of high school and make decisions about post-secondary education and work.

4. Your responses will be merged with those of other students, and the answers you give will never be identified as yours.

GENERAL INSTRUCTIONS

PLEASE READ EACH QUESTION CAREFULLY.

It is important that you follow the directions for responding to each kind of question. These are:

(MARK ONE)

What is the color of your eyes? (MARK ONE)
Brown .... ☐ If the color of your eyes is
Blue .... ☐ green, you would mark the
Green .... ■ square to the right of
Another color .... ☐ green.

(MARK ALL THAT APPLY)

Last week, did you do any of the following? (MARK ALL THAT APPLY)
See a play .... ☐ If you went to a movie and
Go to a movie .... ■ attended a sporting event
Attend a sporting event .... ■ last week, you would mark
the two squares as shown.

(MARK ONE SQUARE FOR EACH LINE)

Do you plan to do any of the following next week? ((MARK ONE SQUARE FOR EACH LINE)

	Yes	Not Sure	No	
a. Visit a relative	☐	☐	■	If you plan to study at a friend's house, do not plan to visit a relative,
b. Go to a museum	☐	■	☐	and are not sure about going to a
c. Study at a friend's house	■	☐	☐	museum next week, you would mark one square on each line as shown.

This questionnaire is not a test. We hope you will answer every question, but you may skip any question you do not wish to answer.

WE HOPE YOU WILL ANSWER EVERY QUESTION, BUT YOU MAY SKIP
ANY QUESTION YOU DO NOT WISH TO ANSWER.

1. Which of the following best describes your present high school program?
    (MARK ONE)

    General .... ☐
    Academic or college preparatory .... ☐
    Vocational (Occupational preparation)
    Agricultural occupations .... ☐
    Business or office occupations .... ☐
    Distributive education .... ☐
    Health occupations .... ☐
    Home economics occupations .... ☐
    Technical occupations .... ☐
    Trade or industrial occupations .... ☐

2. Were you assigned to the program you are now in, or did you choose it
    yourself? (MARK ONE)

    I was assigned.. ☐
    I chose it myself .... ☐

3. Do you expect to graduate from high school? (MARK ONE)

    Yes.. ☐
    Probably.. ☐
    Probably not .... ☐
    No .... ☐

4. When do you expect to leave high school? (MARK ONE)

    Before the beginning of the next school year
    (Before September 1980)... ☐
    During the next school year (September 1980
    to June 1981).. ☐
    After June 1981 but before graduation............................. ☐
    After I graduate .... ☐

5. Do you have a definite job lined up after you leave high school? (MARK
    ONE)

    Yes.. ☐
    No .... ☐

6. During the tenth grade, including all of this school year, how much course
    work will you have taken in each of the following subjects? Count only
    courses that meet at least three times (or three periods) a week (MARK
    ONE SQUARE FOR EACH LINE)

	None	1/2 year	1 year	More than 1 year
a. Mathematics	☐	☐	☐	☐
b. English or literature	☐	☐	☐	☐
c. French	☐	☐	☐	☐
d. German	☐	☐	☐	☐
e. Spanish	☐	☐	☐	☐
f. History or social studies	☐	☐	☐	☐
	☐	☐	☐	☐
g. Science	☐	☐	☐	☐
h. Business, office, or sales	☐	☐	☐	☐
i. Trade and industry	☐	☐	☐	☐
j. Technical courses	☐	☐	☐	☐
k. Other vocational courses	☐	☐	☐	☐

7. Which of the following best describes your grades so far in high school? (MARK ONE)

Mostly A's (or a numerical average of 90-100) .... ☐
About half A's and half B's (or 85-89) .... ☐
Mostly B's (or 80-84) .... ☐
About half B's and half C's (or 75-79) .... ☐
Mostly C's (or 70-74) .... ☐
About half C's and half D's (or 65-69) .... ☐
Mostly D's (or 60-64) .... ☐
Mostly below D (or below 60) .... ☐

8. For each of the high school subjects listed bleow, mark a square for each statement that applies to you. (MARK ALL THAT APPLY FOR EACH SUBJECT)

A. Mathematics
   a. I got mostly A's and B's in this subject .... ☐
   b. It will be useful in my future .... ☐
   c. It was interesting to me .... ☐
   d. Took no mathematics courses .... ☐

B. English or literature
   a. I got mostly A's and B's in this subject .... ☐
   b. It will be useful in my future .... ☐
   c. It was interesting to me .... ☐
   d. Took no English or literature courses .... ☐

C. Business, office, or sales
   a. I got mostly A's and B's in this subject .... ☐
   b. It will be useful in my future .... ☐
   c. It was interesting to me .... ☐
   d. Took no business courses .... ☐

D. Trade or industry
   a. I got mostly A's and B's in this subject .... ☐
   b. It will be useful in my future..☐
   c. It was interesting to me..☐
   d. Took no trade or industrial courses.....................................☐

9. During the 11th and 12th grades, how much course work do you plan to take in each of the following subjects? (MARK ONE SQUARE FOR EACH LINE)

	None	1/2 year	1 year	1-1$^{1/2}$ years	2 years	More than 2 years	Don't know yet
a. Mathematics	☐	☐	☐	☐	☐	☐	☐
b. English or literature	☐	☐	☐	☐	☐	☐	☐
c. French	☐	☐	☐	☐	☐	☐	☐
d. German	☐	☐	☐	☐	☐	☐	☐
e. Spanish	☐	☐	☐	☐	☐	☐	☐
f. History or social studies	☐	☐	☐	☐	☐	☐	☐
g. Science	☐	☐	☐	☐	☐	☐	☐
h. Business, office, or sales	☐	☐	☐	☐	☐	☐	☐
i. Trade and industry	☐	☐	☐	☐	☐	☐	☐
j. Technical courses	☐	☐	☐	☐	☐	☐	☐
k. Other vocational courses	☐	☐	☐	☐	☐	☐	☐

10. Are you now taking or do you plan to take high school courses in any of the following areas? (MARK ONE SQUARE FOR EACH LINE)

	Yes	No	Not certain
a. Agriculture, including horticulture	☐	☐	☐
b. Auto mechanics	☐	☐	☐
c. Commercial arts	☐	☐	☐
d. Computer programming or computer operations	☐	☐	☐
e. Construction trades:			
1. Carpentry, cabinet making, or millwork	☐	☐	☐
2. Electrical	☐	☐	☐
3. Masonry	☐	☐	☐
4. Plumbing	☐	☐	☐
f. Cosmetology, hairdressing, or barbering	☐	☐	☐
g. Drafting	☐	☐	☐
h. Electronics	☐	☐	☐
i. Home economics, including dietetics and child care	☐	☐	☐

j. Machine shop ....☐ .... ☐ .... ☐ ....
k. Medical or dental assisting ....☐ .... ☐ .... ☐ ....
l. Practical nursing ....☐ .... ☐ .... ☐ ....
m. Quantity food occupations ....☐ .... ☐ .... ☐ ....
n. Sales or merchandising ....☐ .... ☐ .... ☐ ....
o. Secretarial, stenographic, typing, or
    other office work ....☐ .... ☐ .... ☐ ....
p. Welding ....☐ .... ☐ .... ☐ ....

11. Since you started the 5th grade, about how many times have you changed schools because you or your family moved? (MARK ONE)

Never ....☐
Once ....☐
Twice...☐
Three times or more..☐

12. Did you go to kindergarten before you started the first grade? (MARK ONE)

Yes...☐
No ....☐

13. Have you ever been in any of the following kinds of courses or programs in high school? (MARK ONE SQUARE FOR EACH LINE)

	No	Yes
a. Remedial English (sometimes called basic or essential)	☐	☐
b. Remedial Mathematics(sometimes called basic or essential)	☐	☐
c. Advanced or honors program in English	☐	☐
d. Advanced or honors program in Mathematics	☐	☐
e. Bilingual or bicultural program	☐	☐
f. Family life or sex education	☐	☐
g. Alcohol or drug abuse education	☐	☐
h. Special program for the educationally handicapped	☐	☐
i. Special program for the physically handicapped	☐	☐

14. Have you ever heard of or participated in any of the following high school educational programs? (MARK ONE SQUARE FOR EACH LINE)

	Never heard of this program	Have heard of this program but have not participated	Have participated in this program
a. Cooperative Vocational Education Program (Co-op Program)	☐	☐	☐
b. High School Vocational Education Work-Study Program	☐	☐	☐

   c. Talent Search .... □ .... □ .... □ ....
   d. Upward Bound .... □ .... □ .... □ ....
   e. Continuation High School .... □ .... □ .... □ ....
   f. Alternative High School .... □ .... □ .... □ ....
   g. Special School for pregnant girls
      or mothers .... □ .... □ .... □ ....
   h. CETA Work Programs (such as the
      Youth Employment and Training
      Program or the Conservation Corps) ..... □ .... □ .... □ ....
   i. Junio ROTC .... □ .... □ .... □ ....

15. Approximately what is the average amount of time you spend on home-work a week? (MARK ONE)

No homework is ever assigned .... □
I have homework, but I don't do it .... □
Less than 1 hour a week .... □
Between 1 and 3 hours a week .... □
More than 3 hours, less than 5 hours a week .... □
Between 5 and 10 hours a week .... □
More than 10 hours a week .... □

16. How often do you come to classs and find yourself <u>without</u> these things? (MARK ONE SQUARE FOR EACH LINE)

		Usually	Fairly often	Seldom	Never
a.	Pencil or paper	□	□	□	□
b.	Books	□	□	□	□
c.	Your homework done	□	□	□	□

17. Between the beginning of school last fall and Christmas vacation, about how many days were you <u>absent</u> from school for any reason, <u>not counting illness</u>? (MARK ONE)

None .... □
1 or 2 days .... □
3 or 4 days .... □
5 to 10 days .... □
11 to 15 days .... □
16 to 20 days .... □
21 or more .... □

18. Between the beginning of school last fall and Christmas vacation, about how many days were you <u>late</u> to school? (MARK ONE)

None .... □
1 or 2 days .... □
3 or 4 days .... □
5 to 10 days .... □

11 to 15 days .... ☐
16 to 20 days .... ☐
21 or more.. ☐

19. To what extent are the following disciplinary matters problems in your school? (MARK ONE SQUARE FOR EACH LINE)

	Often happens	Sometimes happens	Rarely or never happens
Students don't attend school	☐	☐	☐
Students cut classes, even if they attend school	☐	☐	☐
Students talk back to teachers	☐	☐	☐
Students refuse to obey instructions	☐	☐	☐
Students get in fights with each other	☐	☐	☐
Students attack or threaten to attack teachers	☐	☐	☐

20. Listed below are certain rules which some schools have. Please mark those which are enforced in your school. (MARK ALL THAT APPLY)

School grounds closed to students at lunch time .... ☐
Students responsible to the school for property damage .... ☐
Hall passes required .... ☐
"No smoking" rules .... ☐
Rules about student dress .... ☐

21. How old were you when you first worked for pay, not counting work around the house? (MARK ONE)

11 or younger.. ☐
12 .... ☐
13 .... ☐
14 .... ☐
15 .... ☐
16 .... ☐
17 .... ☐
18 .... ☐
19 .... ☐
20 or older .... ☐
Never have worked for pay.. ☐

22. Did you do any work for pay last week, not counting work around the house? (MARK ONE)

Yes.................................... ☐
No .... ☐

23. Were you looking for a job last week? (MARK ONE)

Yes.. ☐
No .... ☐

24. When was the most recent time you worked for pay, not counting work around the house? (MARK ONE)

Never worked for pay... ☐

Last week... ☐
Within the past month, but not last week............................... ☐
Within the past 3 months.. ☐
Since school started last fall .... ☐
Last summer... ☐
Before that... ☐

25. How many hours do/did you work a week on your current or most recent job? (MARK ONE)

None, never worked for pay... ☐

1-4 hours per week... ☐
5-14 hours per week... ☐
15-21 hours per week... ☐
22-29 hours per week... ☐
30-34 hours per week... ☐
35 hours or more per week.. ☐

26. How much do/did you earn per hour on that job (your current or most recent job? (MARK ONE)

Have not worked for pay.. ☐

Less than $1.50 per hour .... ☐
$1.50 to $1.99... ☐
$2.00 to $2.49... ☐
$2.50 to $2.89... ☐
$2.90 to $3.09... ☐
$3.10 to $3.49... ☐
$3.50 to $3.99... ☐
$4.00 per hour or more.. ☐

27. Which of the job categories below comes closest to the kind of work you do/did for pay on your current or most recent job? (If more than one kind of work, choose the one which paid you the most per week.) (MARK ONE)

Have not worked for pay.. ☐

Lawn work or odd jobs... ☐
Waiter or waitress in a restaurant or drive-in........................... ☐

Babysitting or child care.. ☐
Farm or agricultural work... ☐
Factory work, unskilled or semi-skilled.................................... ☐
Skilled trade .... ☐
Other manual labor... ☐
Store clerk or salesperson .... ☐
Office or clerical .... ☐
Hospital or health... ☐
Other .... ☐

28. Is your current job (or was your most recent job) a CETA-sponsored job or another job supported by government funds, or is it for a private company? (MARK ONE)

Have not worked for pay... ☐

CETA-sponsored youth employment job.................................. ☐
Other government-funded job... ☐
Private company.. ☐
Other .... ☐
Don't know... ☐

29. At your current or most recent job, about what proportion of the time is (was) spent on training (not on just doing your regular work on the job)? (MARK ONE)

Have not worked for pay... ☐

Almost no time in training .... ☐
Less than one-quarter of the time .... ☐
About a quarter of the time .... ☐
About half of the time .... ☐
More than half the time in training.. ☐

30. In describing your present or most recent job, would you say it is . . . (MARK ONE SQUARE FOR EACH LINE)

	Yes	No	Never worked
a. A place where people goof off?	☐	☐	☐
b. Something you do just for the money?	☐	☐	☐
c. More enjoyable than school?	☐	☐	☐
d. Encourages good work habits?	☐	☐	☐
e. More important for you than school?	☐	☐	☐

31. What is the lowest hourly wage you would be willing to accept for a job while you are still in high school? (MARK ONE)

Below $1.50... ☐
$1.50 .... ☐

$1.75 .... ☐
$2.00 .... ☐
$2.25 .... ☐
$2.50 .... ☐
$2.75 .... ☐
$3.00 .... ☐
$3.25 .... ☐
$3.50 .... ☐
$3.75 .... ☐
$4.00 per hour or more... ☐
Would not accept any job .... ☐

32. What is the lowest hourly wage you would be willing to accept for a job after you graduate from high school? (MARK ONE)

Below $1.50... ☐
$1.50 .... ☐
$1.75 .... ☐
$2.00 .... ☐
$2.25 .... ☐
$2.50 .... ☐
$2.75 .... ☐
$3.00 .... ☐
$3.25 .... ☐
$3.50 .... ☐
$3.75 .... ☐
$4.00 per hour or more... ☐

33. About how much money do you expect to earn from work in the year beginning July 1980 and ending June 1981? (MARK ONE)

None .... ☐
Less than $1,000 .... ☐
$1,000 to $2,999... ☐
$3,000 to $4,999... ☐
$5,000 to $6,999... ☐
$7,000 to $8,999... ☐
$9,000 to $10,999... ☐
$11,000 to $12,999 .... ☐
$13,000 to $14,999 .... ☐
$15,000 or more.. ☐

34. Have you participated in any of the following types of activities either in or out of school this year? (MARK ONE SQUARE FOR EACH LINE)

	Have not participated	Have participated actively
a. Athletic teams — in or out of school	☐	☐
b. Cheer leaders, pep club, majorettes	☐	☐

c. Debating or drama.....................................☐................☐.......
d. Band or orchestra.....................................☐................☐.......
e. Chorus or dance ....☐................☐.......
f. Hobby clubs such as photography, model
    building, hot rod, electronics, crafts ....☐................☐.......
g. School subject-matter clubs, such as
    science, history, language, business, art..............☐................☐.......
h. Vocational education clubs, such as Future
    Homemakers, Teachers, Farmers of America,
    DECA, FBLA, or VICA...................................☐................☐.......
i. Youth organizations in the community,
    such as Scouts, Y, etc....................................☐................☐.......
j. Church activities, including youth groups............☐................☐.......
k. Junior Achievement....................................☐................☐.......
l. Co-op club ....☐................☐.......

35. Please mark whether each of the following statements is true or false for
    you. (MARK ONE SQUARE FOR EACH LINE)

	True	False
a. I am usually at ease in English class	☐	☐
b. Doing English assignments makes me feel tense	☐	☐
c. English class does not scare me at all	☐	☐
d. I dread English class	☐	☐
e. I am usually at ease in mathematics class	☐	☐
f. Doing mathematics assignments makes me feel tense	☐	☐
g. Mathematics class does not scare me at all	☐	☐
h. I dread mathematics class	☐	☐

36. Which of the following people live in the same household with you?
    (MARK ALL THAT APPLY)

a. I live alone...☐
b. Father..☐
c. Other male guardian
    (step-father or foster-father)..☐
d. Mother...☐
e. Other female guardian
    (step-mother or foster-mother)..☐
f. Brother(s) and/or sister(s) ....☐
    (including step- or half-)
g. Grandparent(s) ....☐
h. My husband/wife ....☐
i. My child or my children..☐
j. Other relatives (children or adults)...................................☐
k. Non-relative(s) (children or adults)..................................☐

37. Did your mother (stepmother or female guardian) usually work during the following periods of your life? (MARK ONE SQUARE FOR EACH LINE)

	Did not work	Worked part-time	Worked full-time	Don't Know	Does not apply
a. When you were in high school	☐	☐	☐	☐	☐
b. When you were in elementary school	☐	☐	☐	☐	☐
c. Before you went to elementary school	☐	☐	☐	☐	☐

The next questions ask about your parents or guardians. Please answer for those parents with whom you are <u>now</u> living. For example, if you have both a natural father and a step-father or other male guardian, answer for the male who lives in the same household with you. If you are living with neither, use the category—'Do not live with father (stepfather or male guardian).

Please answer for the same persons in later questions that ask about your father or your mother.

38. Please describe below the job most recently held by your father (stepfather or male guardian), even if he is not working at present.

(WRITE IN)_____

Which of the categories below comes closest to describing that job? (MARK ONE)

Do not live with father (stepfather or male guardian) .... ☐
CLERICAL such as bank teller, bookkeeper, secretary, typist, mail
carrier, ticket agent .... ☐
CRAFTSMAN such as baker, automobile mechanic, machinist,
painter, plumber, telephone installer, carpenter .... ☐
FARMER, FARM MANAGER .... ☐
HOMEMAKER OR HOUSEWIFE ONLY .... ☐
LABORER such as construction worker, car washer, sanitary worker,
farm laborer .... ☐
MANAGER, ADMINISTRATOR such as sales manager, office
manager, school administrator, buyer, restaurant manager,
government official .... ☐
MILITARY such as career officer, enlisted man or woman in the
Armed Forces .... ☐
OPERATIVE such as meat cutter, assembler, machine operator,
welder, taxicab, bus, or truck driver .... ☐
PROFESSIONAL such as accountant, artist, registered nurse,
engineer, librarian, writer, social worker, actor, actress, athlete,
politician, but not including school teacher .... ☐
PROFESSIONAL such as clergyman, dentist, physician, lawyer,
scientist, college teacher .... ☐

PROPRIETOR OR OWNER such as owner of a small business, contractor, restaurant owner .... ☐
PROTECTIVE SERVICE such as detective, police officer or guard, sheriff, fire fighter .... ☐
SALES such as salesperson, advertising or insurance agent, real estate broker .... ☐
SCHOOL TEACHER such as elementary or secondary .... ☐
SERVICE such as barber, beautician, practical nurse, private household worker, janitor, waiter .... ☐
TECHNICAL such as draftsman, medical or dental technician, computer programmer .... ☐
Never worked .... ☐
Don't know .... ☐

39. What was the highest level of education your father (stepfather or male guardian) completed? (MARK ONE)

Do not live with father (stepfather or male guardian) .... ☐
Less than high school graduation .... ☐
High School graduation only .... ☐

Vocational, trade, or business .... ⎰ Less than two years .... ☐
   school after high school   ⎱ Two years or more .... ☐

                                     ⎧ Less than two years of college ..... ☐
                                     | Two or more years of college
                                     | (including two-year degree) .... ☐
College program .... ⎨ Finished college (four- or five-
                                     | year degree) .... ☐
                                     | Master's degree or equivalent ...... ☐
                                     | Ph.D., M.D., or other advanced
                                     ⎩   professional degree .... ☐
Don't know .... ☐

40. How much of his life has your father (stepfather or male guardian) spent in the United States? (MARK ONE)

All or almost all .... ☐
More than 20 years, but not all .... ☐
About 11-20 years .... ☐
About 6-10 years .... ☐
About 1-5 years .... ☐
Don't know .... ☐

41. Please describe below the job most recently held by your mother (stepmother or female guardian), even if she is not working at present.

(WRITE IN)_____

Which of the categories below comes closest to describing that job? (MARK ONE)

Do not live with mother (stepmother or female guardian) ....□

CLERICAL such as bank teller, bookkeeper, secretary, typist, mail carrier, ticket agent..□

CRAFTSMAN such as baker, automobile mechanic, machinist, painter, plumber, telephone installer, carpenter...............................□

FARMER, FARM MANAGER..□

HOMEMAKER OR HOUSEWIFE ONLY..□

LABORER such as construction worker, car washer, sanitary worker, farm laborer ....□

MANAGER, ADMINISTRATOR such as sales manager, office manager, school administrator, buyer, restaurant manager, government official...□

MILITARY such as career officer, enlisted man or woman in the Armed Forces...□

OPERATIVE such as meat cutter, assembler, machine operator, welder, taxicab, bus, or truck driver...□

PROFESSIONAL such as accountant, artist, registered nurse, engineer, librarian, writer, social worker, actor, actress, athlete, politician, but not including school teacher ....□

PROFESSIONAL such as clergyman, dentist, physician, lawyer, scientist, college teacher ....□

PROPRIETOR OR OWNER such as owner of a small business, contractor, restaurant owner ....□

PROTECTIVE SERVICE such as detective, police officer or guard, sheriff, fire fighter ....□

SALES such as salesperson, advertising or insurance agent, real estate broker ....□

SCHOOL TEACHER such as elementary or secondary............................□

SERVICE such as barber, beautician, practical nurse, private household worker, janitor, waiter...□

TECHNICAL such as draftsman, medical or dental technician, computer programmer..□

Never worked...□

Don't know ....□

42. What was the highest level of education your mother (stepmother or female guardian) completed? (MARK ONE)

Do not live with mother (stepmother or female guardian) ....□

Less than high school graduation..□

High school graduation only...□

Vocational, trade, or business .... ⎰ Less than two years.....................□
school after high school ⎱ Two years or more ....□

College program .... {
Less than two years of college ..... ☐
Two or more years of college
(including two-year degree)....... ☐
Finish college (four- or five-
year degree)............................... ☐
Master's degree or equivalent...... ☐
Ph.D., M.D., or other advanced
professional degree .... ☐
}
Don't know..☐

43. How much of her life has your mother (stepmother or female guardian) spent in the United States? (MARK ONE)

All or almost all .... ☐
More than 20 years, but not all.............................. ☐
About 11-20 years .... ☐
About 6-10 years .... ☐
About 1-5 years .... ☐
Don't know.. ☐

44. Were you born in the United States? (MARK ONE)

Yes... ☐
No .... ☐

45. How much of your life have you spent in the United States? (MARK ONE)

All or almost all .... ☐
More than 10 years, but not all.............................. ☐
About 6-10 years .... ☐
About 1-5 years .... ☐

46. Are the following statements about your parents true or false? (MARK ONE SQUARE FOR EACH LINE)

	True	False	Does not apply
a. My mother (stepmother or female guardian) keeps close track of how well I am doing in school	☐	☐	☐
b. My father (stepfather or male guardian) keeps close track of how well I am doing in school	☐	☐	☐
c. My parents (or guardians) almost always know where I am and what I'm doing	☐	☐	☐

47. How often do you spend time on the following activities outside of school? (MARK ONE SQUARE FOR EACH LINE)

	Rarely or never	Less than once a week	Once or twice a week	Every day or almost every day
a. Visiting with friends at a local gathering place...	☐	☐	☐	☐
b. Reading for pleasure	☐	☐	☐	☐
c. Going out on dates	☐	☐	☐	☐
d. Just driving or riding around (alone or with friends)	☐	☐	☐	☐
e. Talking with friends on the telephone	☐	☐	☐	☐
f. Thinking or daydreaming alone	☐	☐	☐	☐
g. Talking with your mother or father about personal experiences	☐	☐	☐	☐
h. Reading the front page of the newspaper	☐	☐	☐	☐

48. During week days about how many hours per day do you watch TV? (MARK ONE)

Don't watch TV during week............................... ☐
Less than 1 hour .... ☐
1 hour or more, less than 2................................. ☐
2 hours or more, less than 3 .... ☐
3 hours or more, less than 4 .... ☐
4 hours or more, less than 5 .... ☐
5 or more... ☐

49. How much have you talked to the following people about planning your school program? (MARK ONE SQUARE FOR EACH LINE)

	Not at all	Somewhat	A great deal
a. Your father	☐	☐	☐
b. Your mother	☐	☐	☐
c. A guidance counselor	☐	☐	☐
d. Teachers	☐	☐	☐
e. Friends or relatives about your own age	☐	☐	☐

50. What do the following people think you ought to do after high school? (MARK ONE SQUARE FOR EACH LINE)

	Go to college	Get a full-time job	Enter a trade school or an apprenticeship	Enter military service	They don't care	I don't know	Does not apply
a. Your father	☐	☐	☐	☐	☐	☐	☐

b. Your mother............... ☐....... ☐........☐........☐....... ☐....... ☐.......☐.....
c. A guidance counselor ☐....... ☐........☐........☐....... ☐....... ☐.......☐.....
d. Teachers.................... ☐....... ☐........☐........☐....... ☐....... ☐.......☐.....
e. Friends or relatives.... ☐....... ☐........☐........☐....... ☐....... ☐.......☐.....
   about your own age. ☐....... ☐........☐........☐....... ☐....... ☐.......☐.....

51. Please think of your closest friend in this school who is a sophomore. As far as you know, are the following statements true or false for him/her? (MARK ONE SQUARE FOR EACH LINE)

	True	False
a. Gets good grades?	☐	☐
b. Is interested in school?	☐	☐
c. Attends classes regularly?	☐	☐
d. Plans to go to college?	☐	☐
e. Is popular with others?	☐	☐

52 How do you and your friends in this school mostly feel about these different kinds of students? (MARK ONE SQUARE FOR EACH LINE)

	Mostly think well of such a student	Mostly do not think well of such a student	Makes no difference
A. Students who get very good grades:			
Do you	☐	☐	☐
Do your friends	☐	☐	☐
B. Students who are very good athletes:			
Do you	☐	☐	☐
Do your friends	☐	☐	☐
C. Students who are very active socially:			
Do you	☐	☐	☐
Do your friends	☐	☐	☐

53. How do other sophomores in your school see you? (MARK ONE SQUARE FOR EACH LINE)

	Very	Somewhat	Not at all
a. As popular?	☐	☐	☐
b. As athletic?	☐	☐	☐
c. As socially active?	☐	☐	☐
d. As a good student?	☐	☐	☐
e. As important?	☐	☐	☐
f. As a trouble-maker?	☐	☐	☐
g. As part of the leading crowd?	☐	☐	☐

54. Do you know how to . . . (MARK ONE SQUARE FOR EACH LINE)

	Yes	Not sure	No
a. Apply for an office job in a big company?	☐	☐	☐
b. Arrange an appointment with a doctor?	☐	☐	☐

   c. Choose a school program which will help
      you in college? ....☐............ ☐............☐.......
   d. Apply to a college for admission? ....☐............ ☐............☐.......
   e. Find out about different kinds of jobs?......☐............ ☐............☐.......
   f. Arrange a bus, train or plane trip
      to go out of town?....................................☐............ ☐............☐.......

55. Do you get spending money from your parents regularly? (MARK ONE)

I get a regular amount of allowance..☐
I get money when I need it, but not a regular amount.....................☐
I don't get spending money..☐

56. Have you ever had the following experience? (MARK ONE SQUARE FOR EACH LINE)

		Yes	No
a.	Taken music lessons?	☐	☐
b.	Traveled outside of this state?	☐	☐
c.	Taken dance lessons?	☐	☐
d.	Visited a museum?	☐	☐
e.	Taken an ability test outside of school?	☐	☐
f.	Traveled outside of the U.S.?	☐	☐
g.	Been to a professional ball game?	☐	☐
h.	Been to a rock concert?	☐	☐

57. Please rate your school on each of the following aspects. (MARK ONE SQUARE FOR EACH LINE)

		Poor	Fair	Good	Excellent	Don't know
a.	Condition of buildings and classrooms	☐	☐	☐	☐	☐
b.	Library facilities	☐	☐	☐	☐	☐
c.	Quality of academic instruction	☐	☐	☐	☐	☐
d.	Reputation in the community	☐	☐	☐	☐	☐
e.	Teacher interest in students	☐	☐	☐	☐	☐
f.	Strict discipline	☐	☐	☐	☐	☐
g.	Fairness of discipline	☐	☐	☐	☐	☐
h.	School spirit	☐	☐	☐	☐	☐

58. Does your high school have a minimum competency or proficiency test— that is, a special test that all students must pass in order to get a high school diploma? (MARK ONE)

Yes...☐
No ....☐
Don't know...............................☐

59. Have you taken a minimum competency or proficiency test yet? (MARK ONE)

School does not have such a test .... ☐

Yes...☐
No ....☐
Don't know...☐

60. Did you pass or fail or don't you know the results yet? (MARK ONE)

Did not take such a test .... ☐

Passed ....☐
Failed ....☐
Don't know results yet..☐

61. How important is each of the following to you in your life? (MARK ONE SQUARE FOR EACH LINE)

	Not important	Somewhat important	Very important
a. Being successful in my line of work	☐	☐	☐
b. Finding the right person to marry and having a happy family life	☐	☐	☐
c. Having lots of money	☐	☐	☐
d. Having strong friendships.	☐	☐	☐
e. Being able to find steady work	☐	☐	☐
f. Being a leader in my community.	☐	☐	☐
g. Being able to give my children better opportunities than I've had	☐	☐	☐
h. Living close to parents and relatives	☐	☐	☐
i. Getting away from this area of the country	☐	☐	☐
j. Working to correct social and economic inequalities	☐	☐	☐
k. Having children.	☐	☐	☐
l. Having leisure time to enjoy my own interests	☐	☐	☐

62. How do you feel about each of the following statements? (MARK ONE SQUARE FOR EACH LINE)

	Agree strongly	Agree	Disagree	Disagree strongly	No opinion
a. I take a positive attitude toward myself.	☐	☐	☐	☐	☐
b. Good luck is more important than hard work for success	☐	☐	☐	☐	☐
c. I feel I am a person of worth, on an equal plane with others	☐	☐	☐	☐	☐

d. I am able to do things as well as most other people .... ☐ .... ☐ .... ☐ .... ☐ .... ☐ ..

e. Every time I try to get ahead, something or somebody stops me ☐ .... ☐ .... ☐ .... ☐ .... ☐ ..

f. Planning only makes a person unhappy, since plans hardly ever work out anyway .... ☐ .... ☐ .... ☐ .... ☐ .... ☐ ..

g. People who accept their condition in life are happier than those who try to change things .... ☐ .... ☐ .... ☐ .... ☐ .... ☐ ..

h. On the whole, I am satisfied with myself .... ☐ .... ☐ .... ☐ .... ☐ .... ☐ ..

i. What happens to me is my own doing .... ☐ .... ☐ .... ☐ .... ☐ .... ☐ ..

j. At times I think I am no good at all .... ☐ .... ☐ .... ☐ .... ☐ .... ☐ ..

k. When I make plans, I am almost certain I can make them work ..... ☐ .... ☐ .... ☐ .... ☐ .... ☐ ..

l. I feel I do not have much to be proud of .... ☐ .... ☐ .... ☐ .... ☐ .... ☐ ..

63. How do you feel about each of the following statements? (MARK ONE SQUARE FOR EACH LINE)

	Agree strongly	Agree	Disagree	Disagree strongly
a. A working mother of pre-school children can be just as good a mother as the woman who doesn't work	☐	☐	☐	☐
b. It is usually better for everyone involved if the man is the achiever outside the home and the woman takes care of the home and family	☐	☐	☐	☐
c. Most women are happiest when they are making a home and caring for children	☐	☐	☐	☐

64. During the past few weeks, did you ever feel . . . (MARK ONE SQUARE FOR EACH LINE)

	Never	Once	Several times	A lot
a. Particularly excited or interested in something?	☐	☐	☐	☐
b. So restless that you couldn't sit long in a chair?	☐	☐	☐	☐
c. Proud because someone complimented you on something you had done?	☐	☐	☐	☐
d. Very lonely or remote from other people?	☐	☐	☐	☐

e. Pleased about having accomplished
   something? .... ☐ .... ☐ .... ☐ .... ☐ ..
f. Bored? .... ☐ .... ☐ .... ☐ .... ☐ ..
g. On top of the world? .... ☐ .... ☐ .... ☐ .... ☐ ..
h. Depressed or very unhappy? .... ☐ .... ☐ .... ☐ .... ☐ ..
i. That things were going your way? .... ☐ .... ☐ .... ☐ .... ☐ ..
j. Upset because someone criticized you? ...... ☐ .... ☐ .... ☐ .... ☐ ..

65. During the past month, have you felt so sad, or had so many problems, that you wondered if anything was worthwhile? (MARK ONE)

Yes, more than once .... ☐
Yes, once .... ☐
No .... ☐

66. Are the following statements about your experience in school true or false? (MARK ONE SQUARE FOR EACH LINE)

	True	False
a. I am satisfied with the way my education is going	☐	☐
b. I have had disciplinary problems in school during the last year	☐	☐
c. I am interested in school	☐	☐
d. I have been suspended or put on probation in school	☐	☐
e. Every once in a while I cut a class	☐	☐
f. I don't feel safe at this school	☐	☐

67. Are the following statements about yourself true or false? (MARK ONE SQUARE FOR EACH LINE)

	True	False
a. I have been in serious trouble with the law	☐	☐
b. I am overweight	☐	☐
c. Others think of me as physically unattractive	☐	☐
d. I am popular with other students in my class	☐	☐
e. I like to work hard in school	☐	☐
f. I enjoy working for pay	☐	☐
g. I will be disappointed if I don't graduate from college	☐	☐

68. What kind of work will you be doing when you are 30 years old? (MARK THE SQUARE FOR THE ONE THAT COMES CLOSEST TO WHAT YOU EXPECT TO BE DOING.)

CLERICAL such as bank teller, bookkeeper, secretary, typist, mail
carrier, ticket agent .... ☐
CRAFTSMAN such as baker, automobile mechanic, machinist,
painter, plumber, telephone installer, carpenter .... ☐
FARMER, FARM MANAGER .... ☐

HOMEMAKER OR HOUSEWIFE ONLY... ☐
LABORER such as construction worker, car washer, sanitary worker,
  farm laborer .... ☐
MANAGER, ADMINISTRATOR such as sales manager, office
  manager, school administrator, buyer, restaurant manager,
  government official... ☐
MILITARY such as career officer, enlisted man or woman in the
  Armed Forces... ☐
OPERATIVE such as meat cutter, assembler, machine operator,
  welder, taxicab, bus, or truck driver... ☐
PROFESSIONAL such as accountant, artist, registered nurse,
  engineer, librarian, writer, social worker, actor, actress, athlete,
  politician, but not including school teacher .... ☐
PROFESSIONAL such as clergyman, dentist, physician, lawyer,
  scientist, college teacher .... ☐
PROPRIETOR OR OWNER such as owner of a small business,
  contractor, restaurant owner.. ☐
PROTECTIVE SERVICE such as detective, police officer or guard,
  sheriff, fire fighter .... ☐
SALES such as salesperson, advertising or insurance agent, real
  estate broker .... ☐
SCHOOL TEACHER such as elementary or secondary............................. ☐
SERVICE such as barber, beautician, practical nurse, private
  household worker, janitor, waiter .... ☐
TECHNICAL such as draftsman, medical or dental technician,
  computer programmer.. ☐
NOT WORKING... ☐

69. As things stand now, how far in school do you think you will get? (MARK ONE)

Less than high school graduation... ☐
High school graduation only.. ☐

Vocational, trade, or business .... ⎰ Less than two years...................... ☐
  school after high school   ⎱ Two years or more .... ☐

College program............................... ⎧ Less than two years of college ..... ☐
                                          ⎪ Two or more years of college
                                          ⎪   (including two-year degree)....... ☐
                                          ⎨ Finish college (four- or five-
                                          ⎪   year degree)............................... ☐
                                          ⎪ Master's degree or equivalent...... ☐
                                          ⎪ Ph.D., M.D., or other advanced
                                          ⎩   professional degree .... ☐

70. How far in school do you think your mother wants you to go? (MARK ONE)

Less than high school graduation..☐
High school graduation only...☐

Vocational, trade, or business .... { Less than two years...................... ☐
   school after high school   { Two years or more .... ☐

College program............................. {
     Less than two years of college ..... ☐
     Two or more years of college
     (including two-year degree)....... ☐
     Finish college (four- or five-
      year degree)............................. ☐
     Master's degree or equivalent..... ☐
     Ph.D., M.D., or other advanced
      professional degree .... ☐

Don't know..☐

71. What is the lowest level of education you would be satisfied with? (MARK ONE)

Less than high school graduation..☐
High school graduation only...☐

Vocational, trade, or business .... { Less than two years...................... ☐
   school after high school   { Two years or more .... ☐

College program............................. {
     Less than two years of college ..... ☐
     Two or more years of college
     (including two-year degree)....... ☐
     Finished college (four- or five-
      year degree)............................. ☐
     Master's degree or equivalent..... ☐
     Ph.D., M.D., or other advanced
      professional degree .... ☐

72. Did you expect to go to college when you were in the following grades? (MARK ONE SQUARE FOR EACH LINE)

When you were . . .	Yes	No	Was not sure	Hadn't thought about it
a. In the 6th grade?	☐	☐	☐	☐ ..
b. In the 7th grade?	☐	☐	☐	☐ ..
c. In the 8th grade?	☐	☐	☐	☐ ..
d. In the 9th grade?	☐	☐	☐	☐ ..

73. Whatever your plans, do you think you have the ability to complete college? (MARK ONE)

Yes, definitely.. ☐
Yes, probably.. ☐

Not sure.. ☐
I doubt it... ☐
Definitely not .... ☐

74. If there were a program of compulsory two-year service after high school, with options of military service or community service as listed below, what would you most likely do? (MARK ONE)

Military service with educational benefits afterwards
(such as scholarships for veterans) ....☐
Public service (such as hospitals, Peace Corps,
forest service) ....☐
I am undecided...☐
I would try to avoid either option ....☐

75. What is the <u>one</u> thing that most likely will take the largest share of your time in the year after you leave high school? (MARK ONE)

Working full time..☐
Entering an apprenticeship or on-the-job training program.......................☐
Going into regular military service (or service academy)...........................☐
Being a full-time homemaker..☐
Taking vocational or technical courses at a trade or
business school full time or part time ....☐
Taking <u>academic courses</u> at a junior or community college
full time or part time ....☐
Taking <u>technical or vocational</u> subjects at a junior
or community college full time or part time ....☐
Attending a four-year college or university full time
or part time ....☐
Working part time, but not attending school or college ....☐
Other (travel, take a break, no plans)..☐

76. What other things do you now plan to do the year after you leave high school? (MARK ALL THAT APPLY)

a. Work..☐
b. Enter an apprenticeship or on-the-job training program.............☐
c. Go into regular military service (or service academy)..................☐
d. Be a homemaker...☐
e. Take vocational or technical courses at a trade or
business school ....☐
f. Take academic courses at a junior or community college.............☐
g. Take technical or vocational subjects at a junior or
community college...☐
h. Attend a four-year college or university......................................☐
i. Other (travel, take a break, no plans)...☐

77. Assume you are in this situation. You want to go to college but the college you want to attend will cost $1,500 more than you and your family and any scholarship funds can provide. Which one of these would you most likely do? (MARK ONE)

Try to get a loan...☐
Try to get a part-time job..☐
Choose a college that costs less ....☐
Go to college later when funds
  are available..☐
Don't know...☐

78. At what age do you expect to . . . (MARK ONE SQUARE FOR EACH QUESTION)

	Don't expect to do this	Have already done this	Age in years												
			Under 18	18	19	20	21	22	23	24	25	26	27	28	29	30 or more
a. Get married?	☐	☐	☐	☐	☐	☐	☐	☐	☐	☐	☐	☐	☐	☐	☐
b. Have your first child?	☐	☐	☐	☐	☐	☐	☐	☐	☐	☐	☐	☐	☐	☐	☐
c. Start your first regular (not summer) job?	☐	☐	☐	☐	☐	☐	☐	☐	☐	☐	☐	☐	☐	☐	☐
d. Live in your own home or apartment?	☐	☐	☐	☐	☐	☐	☐	☐	☐	☐	☐	☐	☐	☐	☐
e. Finish your full-time education?	☐	☐	☐	☐	☐	☐	☐	☐	☐	☐	☐	☐	☐	☐	☐

79. Is there a particular person of the opposite sex with whom you go out regularly, or with whom you are going steady (or are engaged)? (MARK ONE)

Yes...☐
No ....☐

80. How many children altogether do you eventually expect to have? (MARK ONE)

None ....☐
One ....☐
Two..☐
Three...☐
Four or more...☐

81. Would you consider having a child if you weren't married? (MARK ONE)

Yes...☐
Maybe..☐
No ....☐

82. Suppose a friend asked you about information on methods of birth control. How much information would you be able to give him/her? (MARK ONE)

Very little .... ☐
Some .... ☐
A lot .... ☐

83. Which of the following is your most important source of information about methods of birth control? (MARK ONE)

School courses on sex (family) education .... ☐
Talking with my father or mother........................ ☐
Talking with friends.. ☐
Books and magazines I have read........................ ☐
Clinic or agency .... ☐
I don't know about methods of birth control .... ☐

Background information . . .

84. Sex: (MARK ONE)

Male .... ☐
Female .... ☐

85. Age: (MARK ONE)

13 or younger	14	15	16	17	18	19	20	21 or older
☐	☐	☐	☐	☐	☐	☐	☐	☐

86. Height: (MARK THE SQUARES WHICH INDICATE YOUR HEIGHT IN FEET AND INCHES)

	3	4	5	6	7						
Feet:	☐	☐	☐	☐	☐						

	0	1	2	3	4	5	6	7	8	9	10	11
Inches:	☐	☐	☐	☐	☐	☐	☐	☐	☐	☐	☐	☐

87. Weight: (MARK THE SQUARE THAT INDICATES YOUR WEIGHT)

Less than 100 pounds.. ☐
101-105.. ☐
106-110.. ☐
111-115.. ☐
116-120.. ☐
121-125.. ☐
126-130.. ☐
131-135.. ☐
136-140.. ☐
141-145.. ☐

146-150 .... ☐
151-155 .... ☐
156-160 .... ☐
161-165 .... ☐
166-170 .... ☐
171-175 .... ☐
176-180 .... ☐
181-185 .... ☐
186-190 .... ☐
191-195 .... ☐
196-200 .... ☐
201-205 .... ☐
206-210 .... ☐
211-215 .... ☐
216-220 .... ☐
221-225 .... ☐
Over 226 pounds .... ☐

88. Do you have any of the following conditions? (MARK ALL THAT APPLY)

   a. Specific learning disability .... ☐
   b. Visual handicap .... ☐
   c. Hard of hearing .... ☐
   d. Deafness .... ☐
   e. Speech disability .... ☐
   f. Orthopedic handicap .... ☐
   g. Other health impairment .... ☐

89. Do you feel that you have a physical condition that limits the kind or amount of work you can do on a job, or affects your chances for more education? (MARK ONE)

   No .... ☐
   Yes .... ☐

90. What is your race? (MARK ONE)

   Black .... ☐
   White .... ☐
   American Indian or Alaskan Native .... ☐
   Asian or Pacific Islander .... ☐
   Other .... ☐

91. What is your origin or descent? (If more than one, please mark below the one you consider the <u>most important</u> part of your background.) (MARK ALL THAT APPLY)

HISPANIC OR SPANISH

   Mexican, Mexican-American, Chicano .... ☐
   Cuban, Cubano .... ☐

Puerto Rican, Puertorriqueno or Boricua.................................☐
Other Latin American, Latino, Hispanic, or Spanish descent......☐

NON-HISPANIC

African ....☐
  Afro-American ....☐
  West Indian or Carribean...☐
Alaskan Native ....☐
American Indian..☐
Asian or Pacific Islander ....☐
  Chinese..☐
  Filipino ....☐
  Indian, Pakistani or other South Asian............................☐
  Japanese...☐
  Korean...☐
  Vietnamese...☐
  Other Pacific Islander ....☐
  Other Asian ....☐
European...☐
  English or Welsh...☐
  French ....☐
  German ....☐
  Greek ....☐
  Irish...☐
  Italian..☐
  Polish ....☐
  Portuguese ....☐
  Russian ....☐
  Scottish ....☐
  Other European...☐
Canadian (French)..☐
Canadian (Other)..☐
United States only...☐

Other (WRITE IN)_____ ....☐

NOTE: The following four questions pertain to fundamental freedoms of expression. These and other questions will provide helpful information for the interpretation of survey results. If you have any reservations about answering questions 92, 93, 94 and 95 please remember that you may leave them unanswered.

92. What is your religious background? (MARK ONE)

Baptist...☐
Methodist...☐
Lutheran..☐
Presbyterian...☐
Episcopalian ....☐

Other Protestant denomination .... ☐
Catholic .... ☐
Other Christian .... ☐
Jewish .... ☐
Other religion .... ☐
None .... ☐

93. In the past year, about how often have you attended religious services? (MARK ONE)

More than once a week .... ☐
About once a week .... ☐
Two or three times a month .... ☐
About once a month .... ☐
Several times a year or less .... ☐
Not at all .... ☐

94. Do you think of yourself as a religious person? (MARK ONE)

Yes, very .... ☐
Yes, somewhat .... ☐
No, not at all .... ☐

95. How would you describe your political beliefs? (MARK ONE)

Conservative or very conservative .... ☐
Moderate .... ☐
Liberal .... ☐
Very liberal or radical .... ☐
None .... ☐
Don't know .... ☐

96. Did anyone at home read to you when you were young before you started school? (MARK ONE)

Never .... ☐
Less than once a month .... ☐
One to four times a month .... ☐
Several times a week .... ☐
Every day .... ☐
Don't remember .... ☐

97. How many brothers and sisters do you have in each of the age groups below? Please include step-brothers and step-sisters if they live, or have lived, in your home? (MARK ONE SQUARE FOR EACH LINE)

How many brothers and sisters do you have who are . . .	None	One	Two	Three	Four	Five or more
a. Three or more years older than you	☐	☐	☐	☐	☐	☐
b. 1-2 years older	☐	☐	☐	☐	☐	☐

c. Same age as you.................... ☐.......☐.......☐.......☐.......☐.......☐....
d. 1-2 years younger................. ☐.......☐.......☐.......☐.......☐.......☐....
e. Three or more years younger☐.......☐.......☐.......☐.......☐.......☐....

98. Do you have a twin brother or twin sister? (MARK ONE)

Yes..☐
No...☐

99. American families are divided below into three equal groups according to how much money the family makes in a year. Mark the square for the group which comes closest to the amount of money your family makes in a year. (MARK ONE)

1/3 of American families make: $11,999 or less .... ☐
1/3 of American families make: $12,000 to $19,999 .... ☐
1/3 of American families make: $20,000 or more .... ☐

100. This time families are divided into seven groups according to how much money they make in a year. Mark the square for the group which comes closest to the amount of money your family makes in a year. (MARK ONE)

$6,999 or less..☐
$7,000 to $11,999..☐
$12,000 to $15,999...☐
$16,000 to $19,999...☐
$20,000 to $24,999...☐
$25,000 to $37,999...☐
$38,000 or more...☐

101. Does your family own or rent the house or apartment in which you now live? (MARK ONE)

Own..☐
Rent..☐
Other arrangement..☐

102. How many rooms are there in your home? Count only the rooms your family lives in. Count the kitchen (if separate) but <u>not</u> bathrooms. (MARK ONE)

1	2	3	4	5	6	7	8	9	10 or more
☐	☐	☐	☐	☐	☐	☐	☐	☐	☐

103. Which of the following do you have in your home? (MARK ONE SQUARE FOR EACH LINE)

	Have	Do not have
a. A specific place for study	☐	☐
b. A daily newspaper	☐	☐

c. Encyclopedia or other reference books .... ☐ .... ☐ ....
d. Typewriter .... ☐ .... ☐ ......
e. Electric dishwasher .... ☐ .... ☐ ......
f. Two or more cars or trucks that run .... ☐ .... ☐ ......
g. More than 50 books .... ☐ .... ☐ ......
h. A room of your own .... ☐ .... ☐ ......
i. Pocket calculator .... ☐ .... ☐ ......

104. When you were in the first, sixth, and ninth grades, about how many of the students in your class were <u>Black</u>? (MARK ONE SQUARE FOR EACH LINE)

	None	Few	About half	Most	All
a. In my first grade	☐	☐	☐	☐	☐
b. In my sixth grade	☐	☐	☐	☐	☐
c. In my ninth grade	☐	☐	☐	☐	☐

105. When you were in the first, sixth, and ninth grades, about how many of the students in your class were <u>Hispanic</u> (Mexican, Cuban, Puerto Rican, Latino, or other Spanish descent)? (MARK ONE SQUARE FOR EACH LINE)

	None	Few	About half	Most	All
a. In my first grade	☐	☐	☐	☐	☐
b. In my sixth grade	☐	☐	☐	☐	☐
c. In my ninth grade	☐	☐	☐	☐	☐

106. If you were to go to a trade or vocational school, what field would you most likely train for? (MARK ONE)

Don't plan to go to trade or vocational school .... ☐
Agriculture, including horticulture .... ☐
Auto mechanics .... ☐
Commercial arts .... ☐
Computer programming or computer operations .... ☐
Construction trades: .... ☐
  Carpentry, cabinet making, or millwork .... ☐
  Electrical .... ☐
  Masonry .... ☐
Plumbing .... ☐
Cosmetology, hairdressing, or barbering .... ☐
Drafting .... ☐
Electronics .... ☐
Home economics, including dietetics and child care .... ☐
Machine shop .... ☐
Medical or dental assisting .... ☐
Practical nursing .... ☐
Quantity food occupations .... ☐
Sales or merchandising .... ☐

Secretarial, stenographic, typing or other office work .... ☐
Welding ....☐
Other ....☐

107. If you went to college, would it most likely be . . . (MARK ONE)

A four-year college or university .... ☐
A two-year junior or community college .... ☐

108. If you went to college, would you most likely go to . . . (MARK ONE)

A public college or university .... ☐
A private college or university .... ☐

109. If you went to college, would you probably go . . . (MARK ONE)

In this state .... ☐
In another state .... ☐

110. If you went to college would you probably go . . . (MARK ONE)

Full-time .... ☐
Part-time .... ☐

111. How much do you think each of the following kinds of schooling would cost for a year? Just answer about expenses for tuition, fees, books, and so on — not living expenses. (MARK ONE SQUARE FOR EACH LINE)

Schooling expenses would be . . .

	Under $500	$500-$1,000	$1,001-$2,000	$2,001-$3,000	$3,001-$5,000	$5,001-$7,000	Don't know
a. Cost at a public junior or community college	☐	☐	☐	☐	☐	☐	☐
b. Cost at a state four-year college or university	☐	☐	☐	☐	☐	☐	☐
c. Cost at a private four-year college or university	☐	☐	☐	☐	☐	☐	☐

112. Do you plan to go to college at some time in the future? (MARK ONE)

Yes, right after high school .... ☐
Yes, after staying out one year .... ☐
Yes, after a longer period out of school .... ☐
Don't know .... ☐
No .... ☐

113. Indicate the field that <u>comes closest</u> to what you would <u>most</u> like to study, in college. (MARK ONE)

Agriculture (for example, agricultural economics, agronomy, forestry, and soils) .... ☐

Architecture .... ☐

Art (for example, art, appreciation, design, drawing, photography, graphics, and sculpting)... ☐

Biological sciences (for example, botany, ecology, and zoology) ...... ☐

Business (for example, accounting, business administration, industrial management, marketing, and finance)........................... ☐

Communications (for example, journalism, radio, and television)... ☐

Computer and information sciences (for example, systems analysis).. ☐

Education (for example, secondary education, elementary education, and physical education) .... ☐

Engineering (for example, chemical engineering, civil engineering, electrical engineering, and mechanical engineering)........ ☐

English (for example, creative writing, linguistics, literature, and speech and drama)... ☐

Ethnic studies (for example, Black studies and Mexican-American studies) .... ☐

Foreign languages (for example, French, German, Italian, Latin, and Spanish)... ☐

Health occupations (for example, practical nursing, medical technology, and x-ray technology).. ☐

Health sciences (for example, registered nursing, optometry, and pharmacy)... ☐

Home economics (for example, dietetics, family and child development, and textiles and clothing) .... ☐

Interdisciplinary studies.. ☐

Mathematics (for example, calculus and statistics) .... ☐

Music (for example, music appreciation and composition).............. ☐

Philosophy or religion (for example, ethics, logic, and theology)..... ☐

Physical science (for example, astronomy, biochemistry, chemistry, geology, and physics)... ☐

Preprofessional (for example, prelaw, predentistry, and pre-medicine) .... ☐

Psychology .... ☐

Social sciences (for example, anthropology, economics, government, history, political science, social work, sociology, and urban affairs) .... ☐

Vocational or technical (for example, automobile repair, carpentry, computer programming, drafting, plumbing, stenography, and television repair.. ☐

Other (WRITE IN)_____ .... ☐

114. For students in this school are the following programs available to help pay for further study beyond high school? (MARK ONE SQUARE FOR EACH LINE)

	No	Yes	I don't know

A. Loans:
- a. National Direct Student Loan Program ....☐ .... ☐ ....☐ ....
- b Federal Guaranteed Student Loan Program ....☐ .... ☐ ....☐ ....
- c. Nursing Student Loan Program ....☐ .... ☐ ....☐ ....
- d. State Student Loan Program ....☐ .... ☐ ....☐ ....
- e. College or University Student Loan Program ....☐ .... ☐ ....☐ ....
- f. Regular Bank Loan ....☐ .... ☐ ....☐ ....

B. Scholarships, Fellowships and Grants:
- a. Basic Educational Opportunity Grant (BEOG) ....☐ .... ☐ ....☐ ....
- b Supplemental Educational Opportunity Grant ....☐ .... ☐ ....☐ ....
- c. ROTC Scholarship ....☐ .... ☐ ....☐ ....
- d. Social Security Benefits for Children of Retired, Disabled or Deceased Parents ....☐ .... ☐ ....☐ ....
- e. Nursing Scholarship Program ....☐ .... ☐ ....☐ ....
- f. Veterans Administration Survivors' and Dependents Educational Assistance Program ....☐ .... ☐ ....☐ ....
- g. Veterans' Educational Assistance Program (VEAP) ....☐ .... ☐ ....☐ ....
- h. State Scholarship Program ....☐ .... ☐ ....☐ ....
- i. College or University Scholarship..........☐ .... ☐ ....☐ ....
- j. Scholarships from Private Organizations ....☐ .... ☐ ....☐ ....
- k. Division of Vocational Rehabilitation Educational Benefits ....☐ .... ☐ ....☐ ....

C. Work Programs:
- a. CETA-Sponsored Youth Employment Development ....☐ .... ☐ ....☐ ....
- b College Work-Study ....☐ .... ☐ ....☐ ....
- c. Cooperative Education Program (Co-op Ed.) ....☐ .... ☐ ....☐ ....